Additional Praise For
Serial Innovators

"*Serial Innovators* deals with the fascinating problem of corporate aging and survival. Older firms have lower profitability and higher costs, they command smaller market shares, and have poorer governance, on average. The puzzle is why they are unable to reinvent themselves. Unlike many earlier books addressing this issue, *Serial Innovators* reviews the insights generated in various academic fields and uses that information to offer solutions. The result is a truly inspiring read."

—Claudio Loderer
Professor, Institut für Finanzmanagement
University of Berne, Switzerland

"*Serial Innovators* is a book about the leadership legacies that help firms create lasting value. It is two books in one: a book about the firms that survive for long periods, how they innovate, and how they adapt to changing markets; and also the fascinating story of a new CEO and his efforts to lead his firm through new challenges and to keep his life in balance. It is about how leaders can become better leaders. Nothing more important to read these days."

—Mario Greco
Chief Executive Officer, General Insurance
Zurich Financial Services Ltd

"One of the great mysteries of business and economics is why high performance is so fleeting. Why, like empires, do companies rise to great success, and then fall when they fail to adapt to changes in their environment? In this engaging book, Claudio Feser sheds new light on this age-old question. He finds that there are a few companies—serial innovators—that beat the odds, bounce back from adversity, innovate, and adapt to ever-changing markets. A must read for business leaders in any industry."

—Eric Beinhocker
Author, *The Origin of Wealth*

"How often do you read a book that is academically thorough, utterly practical, entertaining, and inspiring? Drawing on a wide range of research, *Serial Innovators* tells the story of a young CEO going through both a personal and a company transformation. It is a story of leadership. It is a story of legacy. It is a story of life."

—Thomas Gutzwiller
Professor, Executive School of Management,
Technology and Law
University of St. Gallen

"Companies are like biological organisms. They are born, they grow, they mature, they age, and they die. For most companies, this cycle is extremely short—a few years. For some it's about a generation. But only a few achieve a cycle that mirrors the human life span. This book is about what makes companies go stale and what to do about it. In my capacity as chairman of getAbstract, I've read thousands of business books. This one is unique. Feser is not only a brilliant business thinker, he is also a great storyteller. Read this book and you will be enlightened."

—Rolf Dobelli
Chairman, getAbstract
and Author, *Die Kunst des klaren Denkens*

"Creating shareholder value is not the only 'raison d'être' of corporations, firms, and businesses. Companies should positively impact society and make the world a better place. It's about making life better, safer, and healthier. And it's about people and leaders going through personal and professional transformation. This book provides invaluable insights on how to build companies that succeed in today's global, complex, and fast-changing markets."

—Bruno Pfister
Chief Executive Officer
Swiss Life Holding Ltd

"This work draws on an unusually wide set of disciplines—new and old—to shed light on the behavior of organizations and their leaders. Embracing complexity and unpredictability—rather than assuming them away—*Serial Innovators* is a renaissance person's guide to leadership and institution building."

—Bill Huyett
Director, McKinsey & Company
and Co-Author, *Value*

SERIAL
INNOVATORS

SERIAL
INNOVATORS

FIRMS THAT **CHANGE** THE WORLD

CLAUDIO FESER

WILEY

John Wiley & Sons, Inc.

Published by John Wiley & Sons, Inc., Hoboken, New Jersey.
Published simultaneously in Canada.

For general information on our other products and services or for technical support, please contact our Customer Care Department within the United States at (800) 762-2974, outside the United States at (317) 572-3993 or fax (317) 572-4002.

Wiley also publishes its books in a variety of electronic formats. Some content that appears in print may not be available in electronic books. For more information about Wiley products, visit our web site at www.wiley.com.

Library of Congress Cataloging-in-Publication Data:

Feser, Claudio.
    Serial innovators : firms that change the world / Claudio Feser.
       p. cm.
    Includes bibliographical references and index.
    ISBN 978-1-118-14992-8 (cloth); ISBN 978-1-118-17404-3 (ebk);
    ISBN 978-1-118-17405-0 (ebk); ISBN 978-1-118-17406-7 (ebk)
    1. Technological innovations.   2. Creative ability in business.   I. Title.
    HD45.F435 2012
    338′.064—dc23

                                                                2011029125

Printed in the United States of America

10   9   8   7   6   5   4   3   2   1

To Evelyne, Dario, and Alessio

Contents

Foreword

From time to time—not very often—a book about business offers a genuinely new perspective on issues that confront us all. *Serial Innovators* is such a book.

Companies are facing a number of challenges: a dynamic market environment with ever increasing competitive pressure; increased shareholder, employee, and community expectations; activist demands; and more severe regulatory requirements. Keeping a large and global organization innovative and adaptive in such a context requires a great deal of professional competence and drive, an understanding of market opportunities and threats, and an understanding of the capabilities and limitations of the organization and of oneself.

Business always implies risk taking, which in turn implies the danger of failing. This means that companies and their leaders are inherently exposed to patterns such as overconfidence, denial, or projections.

One may expect that these defense mechanisms occur only in companies in crisis and not in times of great success. But when there is praise from all sides and no shortage of recognition, companies and their leaders may fall victim to losing their sense of reality. Successful, admired, and praised organizations can easily become self-centered and isolated from external information. Rather than remaining realistic and aware of the fragility of success, their leaders may take praise and admiration at face value, egos get inflated, and expectations exaggerated, which sooner or later inevitably lead to failure.

Serial Innovators draws on a wide range of academic research and practical experiences to provide a fact-based analysis of the processes when organizations lose their ability to innovate in an ever-changing context, and develops insights on how company leaders can build organizations that can blossom and sustain growth in today's dynamic and challenging markets.

Serial Innovators is also the story of Carl, a young CEO, faced with the challenges of managing a large and increasingly complex organization. It is a story that opens a window on a world that most people never see: the world of those who lead, under constant pressure, and in a world full of opportunities and risks. They have to be able to make decisions based on incomplete information and sometimes contradictory pressures; they have to act while possibly still having doubts, and they must be able to make difficult people choices. Leaders, however, also have the unique privilege to shape an organization, formulate its mission, create alignment, and instill the passion; they can project self-confidence and energy to improve the lives of thousands, sometimes hundreds of thousands, of people based on the firm's scale and capabilities.

Serial Innovators is a thoughtful and compelling book distinguished by the breadth and depth of its scope. The choice of academic references is extensive and links well with the real-life choices that a company leader has to make in shaping the organization that he leads, based on analytical thinking. The author, Claudio Feser, draws from extensive personal experience and offers food for thought for all those with leadership positions—in business and elsewhere.

DANIEL VASELLA, MD
Chairman, Novartis AG

Prologue

This is an extraordinary book. It addresses head on *the* most critical question facing us. That question is: "How can the organizations we create and populate deliver benefits for customers, shareholders, employees, and society?" This is not a question limited to the interests of business people. The answer to this question will determine the rate of human progress and the health of our societies for us and our children.

The greatest human invention is the ability to organize; the ability of a group of people working together toward a common goal to surpass the dreams of individuals. Innovations such as mass production, large-scale agriculture, the Internet, the sequencing of the human genome would simply not be possible without our ability to cooperate through organization. For that matter, neither would be policing, charity, or government itself. Our ability to create society rests on our ability to organize.

Claudio Feser gets to the heart of this question. What does it take to build organizations that succeed for long periods of time? And what stops us? He confronts the dark reality below the potential. Most organizations fail. They fail to engage their customers. They fail to develop their people and they fail to deliver for their shareholders. Most organizations are short-lived. Set up to achieve a goal, to deliver on a task, they grow and develop. But then eventually they age and die. In a process that resembles a super-fast version of the Darwinian evolution of species, their position in the world is taken over by younger, more nimble, more vibrant organizations. History is full of organizations that were once admired global leaders but now no longer exist, and have been replaced by younger, more dynamic competitors: British Leyland, Lehman Brothers, Digital Equipment Corporation, Enron, to name but a few. And this process of the fall of large, established, often admired organizations and the rise of new ones seems to be accelerating. According to a study by Foster and Kaplan of McKinsey & Company, in 1955 a company in the S&P 500 Index stayed in the index for an average of 45 years, and in 1975, for just 26 years. In 2009, the average was estimated to be just 17 years. Could it be that large and admired firms already carry in them the virus that will eventually lead to their decay?

This seems odd. Why would admired, world-class organizations that genuinely understand their industries, have access to the best technologies, employ the best talent, possess the best assets, have the best capabilities, systematically lose out to organizations that have none of that? How can it be that small, inexperienced newcomers systematically beat large, established, experienced, potent, world-class organizations? Why—in the world of organizations—does David beat Goliath over and over again? And why ever more quickly?

Serial Innovators offers answers to these questions. Building on recent advances in science, it dives into the psychology of the human being and of organizations to explain why organizations develop rigidities that prevent them from adapting and innovating in times of change. And building among others on *Beyond Performance* by Scott Keller and myself, it develops insights and perspectives on how to build organizations that not only perform, but are also healthy: organizations that have the ability to continuously adapt and renew themselves. It also shows how the leaders of organizations play a pivotal role in ensuring that organizations stay healthy, young, nimble, and innovative, and how—in doing so—leaders can build enduring legacies.

Written as a fable about a young CEO going through both a company and a personal transformation, *Serial Innovators* is not only a story about innovation and adaptation, it is a story about leadership and legacy. More importantly, it is a story about life.

COLIN PRICE
Leader of McKinsey & Company's Organization Practice

Introduction

The performance pressure on company leaders today is enormous. It is tough to stay at the top. Leaders work hard focusing on profitability and value creation.

Yet, despite all their efforts, value creation by most firms is short-lived. In fact, the whole life cycle of most firms is not very long. The average life expectancy of a firm is roughly 15 years, and only 5 out of 100 live longer than 50 years. Set up on the back of an innovative idea, firms grow and develop, and sometimes they blossom into admired, world-class organizations. But eventually—as if they were biological organisms—they age and die. There is a large graveyard of defunct firms, including household names such as Texaco, Union Carbide, RCA, General Foods, British Leyland, Pan Am, Uniroyal, Bethlehem Steel, Westinghouse, Commodore, Lehman Brothers, Trans World Airlines, Digital Equipment Corporation, Polaroid Corporation, WorldCom, and Enron.

The signs of aging vary from firm to firm. Some firms become blinded by success and begin to resist external views and challenges. Some are locked into mental models and become driven by habits. Some lose the sense of purpose that pervaded them in the early days. Some become bureaucratic. Some have processes and incentive systems that have put them on an autopilot, leading in a dangerous direction. Some develop dysfunctional organizational cultures. The process of aging is subtle, silent, stealthy, and pervasive. As firms age, they struggle to keep up with changing markets, and in today's dynamic markets slow adapters often become big losers. As a consequence, firms get taken over or go bankrupt. They die. Life is ephemeral even for firms.

Sometimes, however, but only sometimes, firms resist the process of aging and rise above this. They adapt and thrive in dynamic markets, they continuously reinvent themselves, and they change their industries. They become serial innovators. Sometimes—by continuously inventing new products and services that make life healthier, better, safer—they change the world. These firms create value for decades, for their customers, their shareholders, and their employees.

This book studies the aging of firms and the factors affecting it. It also uncovers the secrets of building a firm that is a serial innovator, a firm that adapts and thrives in dynamic markets.

It is structured in four parts.

In Part I, it introduces the concept of the corporate life cycle to show that firms, like human beings, are born, grow, mature, and eventually get sick and die.

In Parts II and III, it then studies the factors affecting the aging of firms, the factors that slow down the process of adapting to changes in the marketplace. It reviews the recent findings in relevant academic fields to understand how firms, as they grow and mature, develop rigidities that prevent change. It examines rigidities at two levels: the individual and the organizational.

In Part IV, it uses those findings to uncover the secrets to building a firm that is adaptive, innovative, and can create significant shareholder value for the long term, sometimes for centuries. It is a firm that is driven by the passion to make a difference to customers and society; a firm that is led by learners with an ambitious and positive vision; a firm that is organized and builds on its members' desire to achieve results, and their eagerness to grow and develop; a firm that is quick in developing new capabilities; a firm that, while it focuses thoroughly on execution and results, remains externally oriented and continuously challenges itself. Building such a firm is a challenging task. It is first and foremost an act of leadership.

The book also reflects on the role of company leaders in developing such a firm. It reflects on how leaders can become great leaders who build enduring legacies.

Before we start, let me make three comments.

First, a word on the methodology used in this study. This book is about organizational longevity, continuous innovation, and adaptation. My bookshelf is full of books on great, innovative, and enduring companies, and there is no shortage of advice on how to build such firms. All too often, though, these books sample great companies at a given point in time, and search for commonalities in their strategies and approaches. Few researchers include firms in their samples that might have pursued identical strategies and approaches, but that no longer exist. The findings are therefore subject to survivor bias, a flaw in research methodology. Therefore, if you sort these books by the decade in which they were written, the names of great and enduring companies—and the strategies and approaches used to become one—change from decade to decade.

This book takes a different route. It reviews recent advances in many academic fields that are relevant to organizational adaptation—behavioral economics, psychology, neuroscience, organizational science, network theory, anthropology, sociology, and strategy—and it then attempts to apply these advances to develop insights on organizational longevity. Besides being more robust methodologically, this route makes for more varied, broad reading. The drawback of this route is, however, that the book may be perceived at times to be academic. And in fact, it is easy to get lost in the theory. Some academic material in its original form is such dry reading that it almost makes you feel as if your soul is leaving your body and wandering elsewhere! I have tried to keep the reviews of the various academic areas short, and to focus on the interesting, the practical, and the (hopefully) less obvious business implications.

Second, this book does not pretend to develop a comprehensive framework of organizational longevity, or to teach general truths about the functioning of human beings or organizations. On the contrary, it aims to provide insights, ideas, suggestions, and perspectives—in the full awareness that there are many other perspectives on the matter. It aims to provide stimuli, not definitive answers.

Third, this book is written as the story of Carl Berger. As we will see later, our thinking is guided by stories, by narratives, not by concepts or facts. The story of Carl Berger is fiction. While it builds on some personal experiences, the person and the company described in this book are fictitious, and any resemblance to any existing person(s) or firm is purely coincidental.

Let's now start our journey of discovering the secrets of the serial innovators. But let me first introduce you to our main character, who will accompany us throughout the book: Carl Berger.

CLAUDIO FESER

PART I

The Ephemeral Nature of Firms

CHAPTER 1

Meet Carl Berger

L uke was the driver and general errand runner for the top executives at American Health Devices, Inc. (AHD), a global medical products company based in Trenton, New Jersey. It was an unusually sunny and warm day in November 2004 when he stood nervously at the JFK airport, waiting to meet his new boss.

The last guy, Rittenhouse, was pretty harsh, all business and all boss, never even a smile, so Luke was pretty surprised when Carl Berger emerged, having cleared customs after his flight from Tokyo. This young-looking man, with an open face and dark hair, had to be the new CEO. He'd already nodded and smiled when he saw Luke's AHD sign and he was heading directly toward him.

Luke gulped, "Good morning, Mr. Berger. I'm Luke, your driver."

"Nice meeting you, but call me Carl," Berger said as he reached out for a handshake. Luke then reached for Carl's fine, but worn, leather suitcase, but the new CEO hefted it himself. "I've got it," he said. "Show me where you parked."

Luke appraised his new CEO, getting used to his unassuming manner. To his shock, his CEO seemed to be appraising him, too.

"Thanks for coming to get me, Luke," Carl said. "Have you been with the company for a long time?"

"Five years or so, Mr. Berger," Luke said, as he drove the car swiftly down the road heading toward AHD's offices. "I drove your predecessor, Mr. Rittenhouse."

"Please call me Carl," the new CEO said again. There was no edge to his voice, but still, it was clear how naturally he could exercise authority.

"Yes, Mr. Berger, ahh. I am sorry, I meant Mr. Carl, uh, Carl."

"That's fine, Luke," Carl said. "How are things at AHD? Do you like your work?"

"Working at AHD is a big honor for someone like me, who hasn't been to college. After all, it's one of America's top firms," Luke said.

Carl sat back and enjoyed the view of New York's skyline as they drove toward AHD's headquarters. He was so proud to be back home.

Carl's thoughts wandered to the events of the past few months.

AHD was a leading firm in the global medical device industry. Medical devices are products used for medical purposes in patients, in diagnosis, therapy, or surgery. Products include implantable devices (such as orthopedics, dental implants, optical devices, and hearing aids), capital equipment (like MRI and PET scanners, or X-ray machines), and related supplies.

In 2004, the medical devices industry was fast-growing and highly profitable. AHD was a strong and respected player in three market segments: orthopedic implants, dental implants, and diagnostics.

AHD was a long-standing leader in the reconstructive *orthopedic implants* market. In the late 1970s, due to a breakthrough innovation in coating technology, it had built an enviable market position and reputation with implant products such as joint replacements for hips and knees.

In the 1990s, AHD had seen *dental implants* as a natural extension of reconstructive implants, with a chance to exploit its core product development capabilities and unique manufacturing technologies. Dental implants was a small, niche market. However, given a large unaddressed patient population in industrialized and developing countries, it was growing very fast.

The *diagnostics* market on the other hand was large, mature, slow-growing, and commoditized. Diagnostics companies provide laboratory equipment and supplies to clinical labs, hospital labs, and large specialized labs for tests such as tumor screening and blood testing. AHD, however, focused on point-of-care (POC) diagnostics, which included testing equipment used in practices and clinics, a fast-growing and profitable niche in the broader diagnostic market.

AHD was based in New Jersey, but—with more than 25,000 employees in 40 countries—it was a truly global firm. The board of directors and the management team alone were composed of individuals of 10 different nationalities.

AHD's former president and CEO, Everson Rittenhouse III, always "Mr. Rittenhouse," and usually "Mr. Rittenhouse, sir," had retired in the summer of 2004 without having cultivated any obvious successor. The board of directors had been discussing the succession for almost a year, a period in which it screened several internal and external candidates and deemed them unsuitable for the top job.

In the spring of 2004, Hubert Meyer, the senior member of AHD's board and the head of the nomination committee, had contacted Carl, who was already known in the medical products industry as a young, competitive, and ambitious leader. At the time, Carl was the vice president of marketing and sales and a member of the executive team of KenkoInc in Japan. KenkoInc was a small but very fast-growing orthopedic implants company owned by two Asian private equity firms. It was located in Osaka and had sizable market positions in several Asian markets. Carl had been the vice president of marketing and sales of KenkoInc since its founding in the second half of the 1990s. It was clear to everyone in the medical device industry that he was the man behind KenkoInc's growth and success.

In the spring of 2004, Hubert was traveling in Japan. He visited Carl in Osaka "to talk business," as Hubert put it. Hubert was a tall man in his early sixties and, like Carl, an American citizen. He was soft-spoken, thoughtful, and well-educated. He had made an impressive career in the electronics industry and commanded respect in the broader American business community and the international high tech community for his business acumen, his judgment, and his integrity.

Hubert and Carl talked little business, though. They spent much of their time talking about family and personal matters. This was somewhat surprising, since they had never met before. Carl immediately felt at ease with Hubert, however.

At the end of the day, while they were driving to the airport for Hubert's flight back to the United States, Hubert—almost casually, it seemed—asked Carl, "Would you consider moving back to America to work for AHD?"

Hubert talked about an emerging opportunity to run one of AHD's three divisions, but did not specify which one. The ambitious Carl was obviously very interested, as AHD was 10 times the size of KenkoInc.

"Well," Carl said, "I'm honored by the possibilities your question implies. Joining AHD's management team would be quite an opportunity."

But in the months that followed, Carl heard no more from Hubert and Carl thought that he had probably changed his mind.

Then, six months later, when he had almost forgotten the encounter, Hubert called: "Carl, we are considering you for the position of president and CEO of AHD. Can you meet some of our board members?"

"Wow," said Carl. This was beyond his wildest expectations. All manner of thoughts rushed through his mind, and he had to control his emotions. "When do you need an answer, Hubert?" he asked.

"You have 24 hours; is that sufficient?" responded Hubert.

Carl took a few hours off. He went for a walk in Sankaku Park, close to KenkoInc's head office. He had to sort out his thoughts, to think the matter through. In the evening, he and his wife, Gwen, talked about the opportunity for several hours. In the mid-1990s, Carl had received an offer from two private equity firms to help set up and develop KenkoInc in Japan. The move looked very risky, but Carl saw it as a unique opportunity to accelerate his career. At the time, Gwen had accepted the move reluctantly. It hadn't been ideal for her career as a radiologist, but now after eight years, she loved living in Japan. They had many friends, and their two children, Dave and Alex, were happy, doing well at school, and developing marvelously. Gwen knew what the CEO role at AHD meant to Carl, and she was ready, though certainly not immediately happy, to move the family back to New Jersey.

For as long as he could remember, Carl had worked hard, really hard, for this opportunity.

Carl was a product of institutional foster care. His parents died in an accident when he was four. He grew up in an orphanage in New York, where affection and care were in short supply. Fighting for care makes one competitive. Under an apparently soft-spoken and unassuming exterior, there was a competitive and ambitious Carl. He was always under pressure, under pressure to demonstrate to the world, and to himself, that he was worthy.

Carl's appointment as head of AHD would be the culmination of an impressive career, and an ultimate demonstration of Carl's abilities. To a man in constant search of recognition and admiration, it felt like a triumph.

"After all these years, and these sacrifices, I've got a shot at becoming the head of AHD. This is incredible," he thought.

Carl spoke the following morning with the chairman and the main shareholders of KenkoInc, and they agreed on a way forward. Then he called Hubert: "I would be delighted to interview for the position of head of AHD. Just to be offered a shot at it is a great honor for me. Thank you for your trust in my abilities. When do you want me to come over?"

"Can you be here next week?" asked Hubert.

Two months later, the board appointed Carl as president and CEO of AHD. Despite his success with KenkoInc in Asia, Carl's appointment to the top job at AHD was a surprise to everyone, in the company, in the industry, and in the country. The U.S. media covered Carl's appointment extensively. Some newspapers saw it as a huge mistake. They described the matter as if one of the leading companies in the country had been entrusted to an inexperienced child.

In his early forties, Carl was indeed young and inexperienced. Rittenhouse had retired at the age of 65, after 10 years at the head of the company. Most members of the top management team were in their fifties. Carl had no relationships with any of AHD's important customers. He had no experience in two of AHD's three business lines. And he had not received any exposure to the U.S. medical device market, which represented nearly 50 percent of AHD's sales.

From Day One, Carl's start at AHD was rocky.

After a series of short introductory meetings—with his executive assistant, with the head of the CEO's office (a kind of chief of staff), with the group executive committee (called the Group Executive Team, or GET, for short), and with the staff in the large auditorium of the Trenton headquarters—Carl met with the CFO, Monica, to discuss AHD's upcoming fourth-quarter results.

Monica was Australian. She was highly respected in the investor community. She had been one of the two internal candidates for the top job, but she did not seem to resent the Board's decision. Her short hair, clipped Aussie accent, and severe suits bespoke serious competence, an impression soon undermined by the unfolding of events.

"The estimates of the earnings for the last quarter of 2004 show a 38 percent decline from last year," Monica had told Carl shortly after he took office. She continued: "This is due to adverse exchange-rate movements, and to some hypercompetitive moves at the edge of legality by some of our competitors. Our underlying position and momentum remain strong. Don't worry, the investors will understand it."

They didn't. On the release of the fourth-quarter results in mid-January 2005, AHD's share price fell by 11 percent.

But the fourth-quarter results weren't the only issue. Just one week later, Carl was informed by Monica of a pending U.S. class-action lawsuit against AHD related to diagnostic instruments sold in the United States in 2002. "We weren't expecting this, Carl. But don't worry, our lawyers believe that we can easily manage it," proclaimed Monica.

When he discussed the matter with a lawyer he trusted, Carl did worry. In 2002, AHD had experienced a serious problem with the quality of the products in one of its manufacturing plants. Nevertheless, knowing that the problem existed, AHD still had delivered faulty diagnostic instruments to customers. Subsequently, AHD had been obliged to recall a large number of products, which had seriously damaged its reputation in the U.S. market. When Carl had interviewed for the top job, AHD executives had told him that the quality and recall matters had been resolved. Now, to his surprise, he found himself confronted with a class-action lawsuit hanging over AHD like the Sword of Damocles.

Nor were the poor fourth-quarter results and the class-action lawsuit the only unpleasant surprises Carl encountered. As he learned more about the company, Carl soon realized that AHD was no longer exactly the lighthouse firm that he and others had thought. It seemed that AHD had lost its edge in the past few years.

AHD had missed several technological developments. The medical device industry was dynamic. Many technological innovations and scientific advances—such as molecular markers for diseases, genomics, electronics, and material science—had vastly expanded the scope of new customer solutions. Unfortunately, this also had greatly enlarged the number of competitors, who were taking advantage of new technologies to make inroads into the industry. Also, AHD had failed to expand into new geographies.

In a dynamic and fast-growing industry, AHD had struggled to keep up, and had grown more slowly than its competitors. It had lost market share in all three product lines and in most of its markets. Since its infrastructure was designed for growth, and for increasing sales and production volumes, profitability was depressed. AHD was hardly making any money.

In early 2005, a Wall Street investment banker visited Carl. The fourth-quarter results had triggered a wide range of market rumors about AHD. There was much speculation about a possible imminent takeover. Deutsche Medizinal-Technik (DMT) AG, a young and innovative German medical device player that had outgrown AHD in recent years, was believed to be preparing a takeover bid for the weakened AHD. The investment banker came to test the waters, trying to understand how the management of AHD would react to a takeover bid.

Carl was frustrated with the situation. He had been successful in developing KenkoInc in Osaka. He knew what it took to compete and win in the medical device industry, but he was not so sure that he knew how to carry out a turnaround for AHD, a company that might soon be confronted with a takeover bid from a competitor.

Carl felt isolated. It seemed that he couldn't count on much help from his colleagues on the senior management team. The welcome for the whiz kid—as he was cynically, but not openly, referred to—from his colleagues in the senior management team had been frosty, to say the least. He had learned in his life that it was an advantage to appear unassuming with people—but now he wasn't so sure. A slightly more intimidating manner might come in handy right about now.

One evening over dinner, Carl shared his frustrations with Gwen. He spoke of his fear that he might become known as the last CEO of AHD, his fear of failing. He asked her: "Will this be the end of my career? I cannot let this happen. But how can I turn AHD around? Why did AHD get here in the first place? How can it be that one of the greatest firms in the medical device industry has become a takeover target? How is it that DMT AG, a much younger and smaller firm, can now threaten the existence of AHD? It is as if AHD, a once young, vibrant, healthy organization, has become old and fragile."

Gwen listened carefully, and Carl's last comment provoked a thought. She told him about a meeting with Carla, an old friend of hers, who was now teaching strategy at Yale. She was doing research on the process of how companies emerge, grow, and eventually die. "She studies the aging process, Carl, and how it affects organizations. Maybe you might find some insights there. Shall I see if I can get a hold of her most recent study?"

The next day, she did. That day, Gwen had also news of her own that she wanted to share with Carl. A prestigious laboratory had offered her an excellent part-time position working on a significant radiology research study. But seeing Carl plagued with doubts and uncertain about what he would do next, she decided she would wait and tell him over breakfast the next day. Carl needed time to think about AHD.

CHAPTER 2

Corporate Life Cycle

Commodore Business Machines was founded in Toronto, Canada, in 1954. It started life as a manufacturer of typewriters but turned to adding machines when the American market was hit by a wave of cheap imports of typewriters from Japan in the late 1950s. It went public on the New York stock exchange in 1962. When, in the late 1960s, Japanese firms started exporting adding machines, Commodore's founder, Jack Tramiel, decided to start producing the recently invented electronic calculator. By the early 1970s, Commodore had a profitable business in consumer and scientific calculators.

In the late 1970s, Commodore acquired a chip manufacturer and entered the home computer market. In 1982 Commodore launched the VIC-20, a home computer with advanced graphics and sound. It became the first home computer to sell one million units, and was followed by Commodore 64, which became the best-selling home computer of all time, with sales of around 22 million computers.

In the mid-1980s, to try to increase market share, Commodore started a price war. The move triggered an internal power struggle, and Tramiel left the company to found a competitor. Commodore brought out the initially successful Amiga series. By the early 1990s, however, Commodore's computers were unable to keep pace with the development of the IBM and Apple PCs. Sales fell, and Commodore, the company that had produced the most popular computer of all time, declared insolvency in 1994.

There are hundreds of stories like of the saga of Commodore. A closer look at why such companies eventually fail will shed some light on the questions facing Carl.

11

Table 2.1 shows two lists. On the left is the list of the top 50 U.S. firms ranked by sales in 1960, and on the right is the same list for 2010. The two lists don't have much in common. In fact, only 14 of the top 50 companies in 1960 (28 percent) retained their status and remained among the top 50 U.S. firms in 2010.

TABLE 2.1   Top 50 U.S. Firms Ranked by Sales

Rank 1960	Company	Revenues 1960 (USD m)	Rank 2010	Company	Revenues 2010 (USD m)
1	General Motors	12,736	1	Wal-Mart Stores	421,849
2	Exxon Mobil	8,035	2	Exxon Mobil	354,674
3	Ford Motor	5,238	3	Chevron	196,337
4	General Electric	4,198	4	ConocoPhillips	184,966
5	U.S. Steel	3,699	5	Fannie Mae	153,825
6	Mobil	3,178	6	General Electric	151,628
7	Chrysler	3,007	7	Berkshire Hathaway	136,185
8	Texaco	2,980	8	General Motors	135,592
9	Gulf Oil	2,721	9	Bank of America	134,194
10	AT&T Technologies	2,640	10	Ford Motor	128,954
11	Esmark	2,443	11	Hewlett-Packard	126,033
12	Bethlehem Steel	2,178	12	AT&T	124,629
13	DuPont	2,143	13	J.P. Morgan Chase	115,475
14	Amoco	2,006	14	Citigroup	111,055
15	General Dynamics	1,988	15	McKesson	108,702
16	CBS	1,956	16	Verizon	106,565
17	Shell Oil	1,828	17	AIG	104,417
18	Armour	1,736	18	IBM	99,870
19	Navistar International	1,683	19	Cardinal Health	98,602
20	Kraft	1,667	20	Freddie Mac	98,368
21	Chevron	1,663	21	CVS Caremark	96,413
22	Boeing	1,555	22	UnitedHealth Group	94,155
23	Goodyear	1,551	23	Wells Fargo	93,249
24	Union Carbide	1,548	24	Valero Energy	86,034
25	RCA	1,486	25	Kroger	82,189
26	Procter & Gamble	1,442	26	Procter & Gamble	79,689
27	IBM	1,436	27	AmerisourceBergen	77,954
28	Lockheed Martin	1,332	28	Costco Wholesale	77,946
29	Sinclair Oil	1,222	29	Marathon Oil	68,413
30	Firestone	1,207	30	Home Depot	67,997
31	ConocoPhillips	1,200	31	Pfizer	67,809
32	GTE	1,179	32	Walgreen	67,420
33	Douglas Aircraft	1,174	33	Target	67,390
34	Sperry	1,173	34	Medco Health Sol.	65,968

TABLE 2.1 *(Continued)*

Rank 1960	Company	Revenues 1960 (USD m)	Rank 2010	Company	Revenues 2010 (USD m)
35	Continental Group	1,117	35	Apple	65,225
36	General Foods	1,087	36	Boeing	64,306
37	American Can	1,059	37	State Farm Ins.	63,177
38	American Motors	1,058	38	Microsoft	62,484
39	Republic Steel	1,054	39	Archer Daniels Mid.	61,682
40	International Paper	1,013	40	Johnson & Johnson	61,587
41	United Technologies	988	41	Dell	61,494
42	Citgo Petroleum	981	42	WellPoint	58,802
43	Uniroyal	967	43	PepsiCo	57,838
44	Rockwell	964	44	United Technologies	54,326
45	Borden Chemical	956	45	Dow Chemical	53,674
46	Eastman Kodak	945	46	MetLife	52,717
47	ARMCO	938	47	Best Buy	49,694
48	Burlington	913	48	United Parcel Service	49,545
49	Monsanto	890	49	Kraft Foods	49,542
50	Alcoa	861	50	Lowe's	48,815

Source: CNN Money.

Thirteen companies (26 percent) that were on the 1960 list have been outgrown and surpassed by firms that were smaller or that did not exist in 1960, and are therefore no longer on the top 50 list in 2010.

Twenty-three companies (46 percent) listed in 1960 no longer exist. I'd call them fallen angels. Once proud, vibrant, successful, market-leading firms, and often celebrated in business literature as excellent firms, they have been taken over or have gone bankrupt.

They include such distinguished firms as Mobil (merged with Exxon in 1999), Texaco (merged with Chevron in 2001), Bethlehem Steel (declared bankruptcy in 2001), Amoco (now also part of BP), Union Carbide (part of Dow Chemical since 2001), RCA (acquired by General Electric in 1986), General Foods (acquired by Philip Morris in 1985, now part of Kraft), and Uniroyal (acquired by Michelin in 1990).

Schumpeter's Ghost

Bidermann Bank, an Austrian private bank, was a fallen angel. The bank collapsed in 1924. The collapse left its president, the Austrian Joseph Alois Schumpeter, bankrupt.

Schumpeter, a former economics and political science professor, decided to return to teaching. He first held a chair at the University of Bonn in Germany, and in 1932 he moved to the United States, where he taught at Harvard. He died in 1950.

Schumpeter was one of the last century's most influential economists. During his years at Harvard, he had a group of distinguished followers and students, including the economist Nicholas Georgescu-Roegen, the former chairman of the Federal Reserve Alan Greenspan, and Robert Solow, who received the Nobel Prize for Economics in 1987.

Schumpeter was one of the proponents of the evolutionary theory of economic development. In his book *Capitalism, Socialism and Democracy,* Schumpeter coined the term *creative destruction* to describe the process of economic development and transformation, in which radically innovative companies enter the market and grow, and established companies decline and ultimately go bankrupt (Schumpeter 1976). His thinking is back in fashion today (the British economics magazine *The Economist* devotes a column on business and management to him).

Two recent studies (Foster and Kaplan 2001; Wiggins and Ruefli 2005) demonstrate the validity of Schumpeter's thinking and shed some light on the fall and death of once-great firms.

In *Creative Destruction* (Foster and Kaplan 2001), Dick Foster and Sarah Kaplan of McKinsey & Company provided empirical evidence supporting Schumpeter's thinking, based on the *Forbes* 100 lists for 1917 and 1987. They noted that of the hundred companies in the Standard & Poor's list in 1917, 61 had ceased to exist by 1987. Of the survivors, 21 had dropped out of the list. Of the remaining 18, only 2, General Electric and Kodak, had outperformed the stock market over the course of eight decades. They hypothesized that to survive, firms need to continuously reinvent themselves, actively cannibalizing existing operating models and existing products.

In a study published in 2005, Robert Wiggins of the University of Memphis, and Tim Ruefli of the University of Texas (Wiggins and Ruefli 2005) examined almost 7,000 companies over a quarter of a century. They found that only five percent of the companies analyzed achieved a period of superior performance lasting more than a decade, and only half of a percent managed two decades. Wiggins and Ruefli noted that "Schumpeter's ghost is alive and well" (Beinhocker 2006).

The two studies show that it is hard for firms to maintain their leading position for long periods of time. Competitive advantage erodes over time, and most firms end up being taken over by younger, more innovative companies.

Eric Beinhocker, a young economist and the author of *The Origin of Wealth,* believes that markets morph continuously. Markets evolve and change as new technologies emerge, as new competitors create new industries and market segments, as regulations change, and as consumers' demands alter. Markets continuously offer new opportunities for wealth creation. Existing firms are, however, slow in capturing them. Set up to implement a given strategy by carrying out a number of business plans, existing firms are slow to shift when circumstances change. It takes time to refocus a large firm on new opportunities. Instead, the new opportunities are captured by new, nimble, fast, and more agile competitors. In short, "while markets are incredibly dynamic, firms aren't" (Beinhocker 2006).

The Corporate Life Cycle and Aging Firms

In two studies published in 2009, Claudio Loderer, and his colleagues Klaus Neusser and Urs Waelchli (Loderer, Neusser and Waelchli 2009), all of the University of Berne, hypothesized that firms go through an aging process; that like humans, firms have a life cycle. Founded on the back of an innovation they quickly establish themselves in the marketplace. Then they learn how to grow and how to capture value. They become more efficient, they find ways to standardize their processes, they find ways to specialize roles in the organization, they learn how to better market their products to their customers. They build knowledge and skills. However, as firms age their development slows, they lose their vitality and momentum, and their knowledge and skills become obsolete. Their profitability deteriorates and, eventually, they die.

Using a sample of nearly 11,000 firms listed on the stock market from 1978 to 2004, they demonstrated that performance deteriorates as firms age and that few firms, if any, survive over long periods of time. Most companies disappear because they are absorbed into other companies.

The life expectancy at birth of a human being in a developed economy today is roughly 80 years. The life expectancy of firms is much shorter. Defining firm age as the number of years since listing, the three economists showed that roughly half of the companies do not live longer than one decade. Only 15 percent of companies survive longer than 30 years, and only 5 percent make the 50-year mark. There are extremely few firms that make it to the millennium. Japan's Ho-shi (hotel), Italy's Marinelli (foundry), and France's Goulaine (winery), were all founded more than 1,000 years ago. (The Western world's oldest continuously operating enterprise is the

Roman Catholic Church, which has existed in its current form since the fourth century. We return to this at the end of the book.)

One of the reasons for the ephemeral nature of firms is that as they grow and mature—unlike biological organisms that suffer from cell death—they appear to develop two kinds of organizational rigidities that prevent them from adapting to fast-changing, dynamic markets (Beinhocker 2006; Loderer 2009).

First, they seem to suffer from what Kaplan and Foster have called a "cultural lock-in" (Foster and Kaplan 2001). Firms that have successfully survived the early years seem to be locked into *mental models* that prevent change. For example, they discontinue new products too early because of fear of cannibalizing important, existing product lines.

Second, they codify their success through *rigid organizational constructs* such as hierarchy, processes, rules of conduct, and standard operating procedures. They seem to be subject to a process of ossification, which results in inertia (Hannan and Freeman 1977, 1989; Leonard-Barton 1992).

In the following chapters, we turn to recent advances in economics, psychology, neuroscience, network theory, organization theory, and strategy to help us analyze rigidities in more detail. We also discuss approaches for addressing them. Our analysis will help Carl. But it will also help us uncover the secrets for building adaptive firms, firms that can shape their industries and society for decades.

We examine rigidities at two levels: the individual and the organizational.

First, in Part II, we consider rigidity at the level of individual members of the organization, for organizations change through the behavior of individual people. We look at three rigidities. First, human thinking is imperfect and biased. Individuals may develop biases that prevent them from recognizing changes in the marketplace. Second, individuals may not develop the self-confidence and perseverance to deal with the changing environment, and therefore give up and get stuck. Third, because of the structure and functioning of the human brain, changing behavior is hard, even if the need for change is understood and accepted.

Second, in Part III, we consider the level of the organization as a whole. Here, we look at five rigidities. First, over time, firms may develop dense hierarchies and complex organizational structures that prevent them from adapting. Second, organizations may lose the sense of purpose that inspired them in their early days, and may fail to engage their members on a common purpose. As a consequence, the divergent interests of these members may slow down the process of adaptation. Third, firms may develop strong cultures that hinder change and adaptation. Fourth, ill-designed incentives may cause people and organizational units to behave dysfunctionally. Last, companies' histories, assets, and existing capabilities are the platforms for renewal, but they may also limit firms' ability to innovate and adapt to a changing environment.

■ ■ ■

AHD had what Carl called a "BS culture." He and Gwen, whose input was his secret weapon, had discussed it several times at home. From the top down to middle management, people didn't seem to talk about content or facts, and didn't show any interest in making decisions or taking action. It was a culture of engaging in long, abstract, inconclusive discussions. The tone of these discussions was always inspirational and positive, and always rich in attributes such as *excitement-oriented, insights-centric, paradigm-changing, pattern-breaking,* or *unrivalled.* Yet nothing was getting done. The execution muscle of the organization seemed atrophied.

Carl saw a vignette of the BS culture during a strategy session with the Group Executive Team (GET) roughly one month after his appointment. He'd had frequent individual meetings with each of its members as he got to know AHD, but he was still trying to understand the group dynamics. He had the strong feeling that something was not working, even though the GET was composed of six experienced and seasoned industry executives, in addition to himself. It included Monica, the CFO (whose office oversaw Human Resources and Legal, as well as Finance), three product unit heads (orthopedics, dental, and diagnostics), the head of manufacturing, and the head of the regional divisions that governed AHD's various national organizations.

The business unit heads were Mark from orthopedics, Luca from diagnostics, and Sergei from the dental division.

Mark was both much more serious and more deeply emotional than his jovial face, frequent grin, and youthful appearance made him seem. He had been the second internal candidate for the top job. Hubert had told Carl that the board decided not to promote Mark because he was too dedicated to orthopedics and its people in both a helpful way (he was an extremely valuable leader in his current role) and a harmful way (his overriding loyalty to his department and his team had always prejudiced his overall view).

Luca, an intense, independent-minded second-generation Italian immigrant, led the diagnostics business unit effectively but with no pretense of sharing decision making with anyone. Slightly stooped but energetic, Luca much preferred working alone. Carl sensed that just having a GET strategy meeting put Luca on guard and made him protective of his prerogatives.

Sergei, an impeccably dressed engineer with Slav roots, led the dental implants business unit. Though an engineer, he had the charm, warmth, and chairside manner of the best dentists. Good with people, oversensitive but smart, he had built a loyal following despite his deep need for constant praise and bolstering—a need Carl was yet to discover.

Arthur and John headed the manufacturing operation and the regional organizations, respectively.

Arthur, a food-loving, hearty native of Provence in France was more rough-edged but also far more truly confident than Sergei, his engineer colleague. While less polished than the other GET members, he understood every nuance of AHD's complicated production processes. He didn't care much for strategy discussions, though; he was a practical budget and schedule man, through and through.

John was a lanky crew-cut former major in the U.S. infantry, where his nickname had been Bullseye. He ran the three regional organizations, Americas, Europe, and Asia, with the precision of a drill sergeant. Focused on his people (troops, he called them) and his divisions (forces), John liked the specialized argot and hierarchy of business. Carl saw him as totally organized and reliable, which he was—if somewhat out of date.

The GET group settled around the conference table. Luca, Sergei, and Mark, the division heads, lined up on one side, faced by Monica, Arthur, and John. Carl watched as the GET members moved almost automatically into their obviously accustomed seats, and he then sat down at the head of the table.

Christian, a young executive whose bustling corporate air made it clear that he saw himself as a hot up-and-comer, facilitated the long-planned strategy session. He was the head of group strategy and—while not a member of the GET—he reported directly to Carl. A few months before the announcement of Carl's appointment, Christian had taken the initiative, with the former CEO's approval, of developing a proposal for a new strategy. Christian launched into the meeting convinced that this presentation would give him a head start with the new boss.

"Hi. Let me introduce myself. I am Christian from the Strategy department. For the past few months, my colleagues and I have brought some blue-sky thinking to work on AHD's new strategy," the young man proclaimed, with a slightly bumptious air.

"First of all, I'd like to say how much of a kick I have gotten out of working with the GET members and our middle management in the last few months. Our company sure has a load of passionate, highly capable, and diverse human capital, and it has been a privilege to work with them. It is clear to me that we at AHD know how to play the game. We at AHD know how to win the game. But we can go further. I believe that AHD can shape the game!" Christian proclaimed.

For Carl, this was all a bit too flashy, but he thought he should listen and give the guy a chance.

Christian continued: "Our strategy department has recently concluded a two-year-long research study on corporate performance over the long term. Using nonlinear multiple regressions and other sophisticated statistical methodologies, we have analyzed the share price performance data of a hundred firms over the last decade, and we validated our findings with detailed analyses of 10 peak performance companies. We have concluded that company success is about winning the hearts and minds of the front-line employees, and about what we call 'synchronicity of management.'"

So far, so good, Carl thought. The expressions "winning hearts and minds" and "synchronicity of management" were vague and jargony, but there was nothing wrong with the concepts. Working as a team at the top and engaging the organization—while a bit simplistic—made sense.

Christian then showed a chart depicting peak companies' share price performance as a function of the "synchronicity factor"—whatever that was. The chart had wrongly labeled x and y axes, and there was an obvious flaw in the data shown, but nobody seemed to notice.

Christian continued: "We are suggesting launching one of the greatest change programs that AHD has ever undertaken. We are going to take the hearts and minds into a whole new ballpark, and we are going to retool their capabilities. Step one is to rebrand AHD and to look for a new identity."

"Oh my God, this really is BS," thought Carl, dismayed—and by BS he did not mean blue sky. This was the biggest attempt to obfuscate common sense that he had seen in a while; he had hoped for something much better. Yet, the GET members continued to listen and seemed to be engaged with Christian's presentation. They showed no resistance whatsoever. Arthur and John requested clarifications here and there during Christian's presentation. And the members held a short, diversionary discussion about the timing of a possible rebranding campaign ("Now or in quarter three?" asked one), and made a few comments ranging from "insightful, and game-shaping approach to energizing the organization" to "exciting ideas, but we also need to think about a game-shaping front-line boot camp."

Carl sat and listened, and the more he heard, the more exasperated he became. Eventually, he stood up, interrupted the presentation, thanked

Christian, and told him that he was done and that he could leave—the takeover was so abrupt that Christian barely had time to pick up his BlackBerry and run.

Alone with the GET members, Carl exploded. "I just don't believe what I've been listening to! This company has serious problems. Our quality is poor; we are faced with a lawsuit; we are losing market share; we have missed several new technologies; our results are bad; there are rumors that we might be taken over—and all we can do is sit around and listen to a presentation about 'synchronicity,' 'game-shaping,' and 'hearts and minds'!"

The members were stunned into silence by Carl's uncharacteristic outburst. For almost two minutes, two very long minutes, nobody spoke, as he stood and glared at them. It was the last time that the expressions "synchronicity," "game-shaping" and "hearts and minds" were heard within AHD.

Carl continued, "We are not going to waste our time on that sort of BS. I am determined to lead AHD back into a winning position in this industry by building on our well-known capabilities. We're good at innovation, distribution, and customer service, but now we have to be better."

He sat down with a sigh. He knew the medical products business, and he knew what it took to be successful in the industry, but clearly he had to bring the GET along. "Let's all get a fresh cup of coffee and I'll share my ideas, instead of letting Chris distract us with his nonsense." Somewhere in the back of Carl's mind, he was already sending young Christian to a regional outpost for a little real work and seasoning under John, the Bullseye's, watchful eye.

As Carl outlined his concepts about improving quality, investing in new technologies, and expanding the geographic footprint, he soon realized that the GET's members were not with him. Their thinking was not aligned with his view of AHD's situation. Nor were they aligned with his ideas; in fact they weren't aligned on anything much at all. The term GET, "group executive team," seemed a gross misnomer: It was a collection of individuals, not a group; nothing was being executed; and the team dynamics—driven by the obviously differing personal agendas of the various GET members—were very poor, despite their surface cordiality.

In the management team, only Monica, the CFO, seemed to support Carl and to share his views. That was because she was very concerned about AHD's profitability. The company's infrastructure was designed for higher sales volumes. Fixed costs were high and there weren't many expenses that could be reduced quickly. Monica was convinced that the company had to grow, or—if it failed to grow—to merge with a competitor.

Mark, the head of the orthopedics unit, was a good man with a superb reputation as a people leader. Fortunately, he didn't seem to resent being passed over for the CEO job, but he wasn't comfortable with any criticism of his orthopedics business. He did not share Carl's belief that AHD's strategy needed revision, in particular in orthopedics.

The dynamics were similar with Sergei, who had been instrumental in building the dental implant business in the 1990s. Much like Mark, Sergei became very defensive when the discussions focused on the performance of his business unit—but he knew that the dental implants team had missed out on a few key innovations in the recent past.

Luca, the head of the diagnostics unit, did not engage very much in the strategy discussion. He was an introverted, lone wolf type, for all of his outward courtliness. "Quite a surprise for someone with an Italian background," thought Carl. Luca's sole focus was the diagnostics business, which had the reputation of being a silo within AHD. Also, he tended to become very defensive and abrasive whenever the discussion turned to his unit's quality problems.

Nor did Arthur, the head of manufacturing, engage much in the team discussions. Arthur focused solely on his manufacturing unit, trying to solve its quality problems. He was not interested in the firm's strategy. He felt it wasn't a matter of concern for him. His job was to produce effectively whatever the business units asked him to. In his mind, it was their task to sort out the strategy. His was to deliver the goods.

John's only concern was the troops in his regional forces. As regimented as if he were still in the army, John was a fervent proponent of the "hey, all is well" philosophy, and saw no problem with AHD's strategy whatsoever. As long as his regional commanders hit their targets and kept their operations battle-ready, he was fine.

Carl's meeting with the GET ended without having reached an agreement on the way forward.

But the members of the GET were not the only ones who did not share Carl's ideas. When he met the board the week after, Carl realized that the members of the board didn't agree with his views either. Most board members, including Hubert, the senior director, believed that AHD's recent misfortunes were due solely to bad luck in launching new products, and that some competitors were believed to have bought themselves into the market, apparently by following unethical sales practices. In their minds, AHD was in great shape and would eventually recover its old form.

Carl was frustrated with the situation. He could not understand how the board and his top team could be so oblivious to the challenges that AHD was facing. In his mind, the facts were clear, and the issues serious. "Why do they not see how bad the situation is? How can they be so blind? This makes no sense. This is not rational!" he thought. He had to figure out how to open their eyes; clearly, ordinary facts and figures weren't enough to do the job.

One evening Carl was driving home after a long day of work. It was late and the roads were empty. He was lost in thought as the radio broadcast a report on the stock markets. That day, prices had risen markedly and unexpectedly on the global stock markets, from Tokyo to New York.

The stock market report was followed by an explanation of the psychology of investing, by a professor who taught behavioral economics at Harvard. He was explaining why humans are sometimes not rational. It was an illuminating and exciting report.

It wasn't the only thing that illuminated Carl that evening, though.

He suddenly saw flashing lights and realized that he was being pulled over by a state police highway patrol car. Immersed in his thoughts and excited about what he had just heard on the radio, Carl hadn't watched the speedometer and had been caught breaking the speed limit.

At first he thought of explaining the situation to the police officer: that he had been concentrating on an exciting and illuminating report on behavioral economics on the radio.

But then he thought that the police officer would probably not share his excitement about behavioral economics. The police officer nevertheless made Carl's economic behavior that evening very simple: "You were breaking the speed limit, sir. The fine for that is 100 dollars."

PART II

Individual Rigidities

CHAPTER 3

To Err Is Human

Imagine that the United States is preparing for the outbreak of an unusual Asian disease, which is expected to kill 600 people. Two alternative programs to combat the disease have been proposed. Assume that the exact scientific estimates of the consequences of the programs are as follows:

If Program A is adopted, 200 people will be saved.
If Program B is adopted, there is a one-third probability that
600 people will be saved and a two-thirds probability that no
people will be saved.

Which of the two programs would you favor? In this version of the problem, a substantial majority of respondents favor program A, indicating risk aversion.

Other respondents, selected at random, receive a question in which the same cover story is followed by a different description of the options:

If Program A' is adopted, 400 people will die.
If Program B' is adopted, there is a one-third probability that
nobody will die and a two-thirds probability that 600 people
will die.

A clear majority of respondents now favor program B', the risk-seeking option. Although there is no substantive difference between the versions, they evidently evoke different associations and evaluations.

This passage is taken from Daniel Kahneman's Nobel Prize lecture for the Nobel Prize for Economics that he received in 2002 (Kahneman 2002). It shows that a different presentation (framing) of identical information can lead to different decisions. We will come back to Kahneman, the leading spirit in the field of behavioral economics, but for now the point is that it seems that people don't always think and act rationally when confronted with choices.

This is a disturbing thought. We like to believe that we are rational, that when we face an important decision—like the purchase of a house or an important career move—we gather all the relevant facts, and then decide rationally.

Neoclassical economics—a period in the history of economic science that spans much of the nineteenth and twentieth centuries and included some of the most influential and acclaimed economists, including Leon Walras, Vilfredo Pareto, J. R. Hicks, Friedrich Hayek, and Paul Samuelson—is largely based on the assumption of perfect rationality. *Homo economicus*—as it describes the rational human being—is perfectly smart, perfectly informed, and perfectly selfish (that is, utility maximizing).

Not That Smart, Not That Informed, Not That Selfish

In the 1950s, Herbert Simon and his colleagues at Carnegie Mellon University, Richard Cyert and James March, started to question the assumption of perfect rationality. Simon and his colleagues did something quite unconventional for economists at the time. They observed how real people, actual managers in actual companies, made real decisions. And what they observed was not *homo economicus* (Beinhocker 2006).

They observed that people's rationality is limited by the information they have, by the cognitive limitations of their minds (how smart they are), and by the finite time that they have to make decisions. Thus, people are *satisficers,* people seeking satisfactory solutions rather than optimum ones. Simon coined the term *bounded rationality* to describe this phenomenon (Simon 1978).

Simon received the Nobel Prize for Economics in 1978. His approach of observing and experimenting with real people became a source of inspiration for many economists and psychologists. In the 30 years that followed, a growing number of economists and psychologists developed a vast body of knowledge and evidence for the not-so-rational human, and created a new research field called behavioral economics.

Two of them, Ernst Fehr, the director of the Institute for Empirical Research in Economics at the University of Zurich, and Simon Gächter, an economist teaching at the University of Nottingham, demonstrated—again with experiments—that humans aren't perfectly selfish, either. In addition to their self-interest, humans also have naturally altruistic inclinations (Fehr and Gächter 2000). Biologists believe that this is the result of evolution, and the fact that collaboration has served humankind well in adapting to a changing environment over the past 100,000 years or so (Precht 2007).

It was time for the super-smart, perfectly informed, and egoistic *homo economicus* to go into retirement. The more modest, more fallible, and more socially oriented human being put forward by the behavioral economists was born.

Rules of Thumb

Let's return to pioneering behavioral economist Daniel Kahneman, an Israeli-American psychologist who teaches at Princeton University. In the 1970s, he and Amos Tversky published a series of research papers that showed how real people's decision making is often flawed and biased.

In Kahneman's 2002 Nobel Prize lecture, he articulated his, and Tversky's, view of human thinking (Kahneman 2002). He distinguished two generic modes of thinking: a rapid, instinctive, intuitive, and automatic mode, which he described as System 1, and a conscious, deliberate, controlled, and reflective mode, which he called System 2. The operations of System 1 are fast, automatic, effortless, associative, and difficult to control or modify. The operations of System 2 are slower, serial, flexible, and effortful.

System 1 steers cognitive processes that do not require much attention, such as speaking one's native language or intuitively catching a thrown ball. System 2, on the other hand, requires real thinking, such as when performing mathematical calculations. Because System 2 is slow, painful (what is 418 divided by 11?), and requires lots of concentration, much of our daily thinking is taken over by System 1.

Also, because the functioning of System 2 is so demanding, and because we have limited time to think and make decisions, our cognitive system often relies on judgment heuristics, that is, experience-based decision rules, such as proxies, or rules of thumb.

In an influential article written in 1974, Tversky and Kahneman identified three heuristics of judgment: anchoring, availability, and representativeness (Tversky and Kahneman 1974).

The *anchoring heuristic* is that we tend to anchor our thinking on whatever information is available, even if it is completely irrelevant. Suppose that you have to estimate quickly the value of something that you are not very familiar with, let's say the price of an aircraft carrier. You have no relevant information, so you *anchor* your decision on the next-best information you have. You read something last week about the cost of building a bridge. So, you take that and adjust upward or downward depending on which object you believe to be more expensive.

Studies have shown that such arbitrary reference points can bias judgment (Tversky and Kahneman 1974). For example, using a randomly selected low number as an anchor will lead people to estimate a smaller crowd in a stadium than will starting with a large number (Bandura 1997). Even completely irrelevant anchors, such as a telephone number given to people in a test, for example, can influence their estimates of a price. Bankers who sell companies sometimes manage to sell at very high prices, in part because they have anchored the buyers on a very high price at an early stage.

The *availability heuristic* is that we assign higher probabilities to events that we can remember vividly, if they are readily available to our brain. How high is the chance of you getting swine flu? Many people in the summer of 2009 changed their vacation plans and chose not to travel to the United States, following several media reports about swine flu–related deaths in the United States. Even though the number of deaths was by any count minuscule, people felt that their lives would be at risk. The *availability heuristic* was at work.

If relevant examples are easily available for people to consider, they assign them a higher probability of occurrence. For example, in the aftermath of an earthquake, sales of earthquake insurance policies rise sharply, but they decline steadily as memories of the earthquake recede (Thaler and Sunstein 2008).

The third of Kahneman and Tversky's original rules of thumb is the *representativeness heuristic,* which is that we develop patterns and stereotypes to categorize information. When people are asked to judge how likely it is that something, such as a car, belongs to one category as opposed to another, they use stereotypes to categorize it.

Many examples of the brain creating misleading patterns exist in investing, where people tend to confuse random fluctuations with causal patterns. If your private banker has guessed correctly for three days in a row whether the equity index would rise or fall, you may believe that this banker knows, or is doing, something unique. Your brain may see a pattern, even though what you have observed is mere coincidence.

In a business context, the representativeness heuristic leads to another problem: *mental models.* Individuals develop stereotypes or mental models over time to categorize information. In particular, as managers spend longer in a firm, and gain experience, they tend to develop a system of stereotypes that allows them to take decisions quickly and efficiently. (If our competitor reduces his prices, we will, too. That will teach him not to do so.)

Experience-based stereotypes can be very helpful, but they can also be enormously dangerous, especially in unfamiliar business situations, such as when—for example—a management team is simply blind to the fact that its industry is going through a fundamental change. The problem is particularly acute in organizations that have a very experienced management team at the top, in which all members of the top team share similar experiences, and thus have similar mental models.

Mental Biases

Although rules of thumb are effective in enabling fast decision making, and efficient, because they require little effort, they also produce systematic *mental biases,* or thinking mistakes. Behavioral psychologists have uncovered and documented dozens of mental biases over the past 30 years.

Let's look at the four of these—framing, optimism, loss aversion, and status quo—as outlined in the book *Nudge* by Richard Thaler, professor of behavioral science and economics, and director of the Center for Decision Research, at the Graduate School of Business of the University of Chicago, and Cass R. Sunstein, professor of jurisprudence of the University of Chicago Law School and Department of Political Science (Thaler and Sunstein 2008).

First, the *framing bias* says that the way information and choices are presented matters. As we have seen at the beginning of the chapter, people react differently if the same information is presented in a different manner. Another powerful illustration of the framing effect is Figure 3.1, which can be found in Kahneman's Nobel Prize lecture.

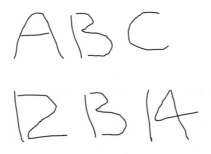

FIGURE 3.1   Context Matters

Source: Kahneman, D. "Maps of Bounded Rationality: A Perspective on Intuitive Judgment and Choice." Nobel Prize Lecture in Stockholm, Sweden, December 8, 2002, 455.

The same information (B or 13) is a letter when presented in an alphabetical frame, and a number if presented in a numerical frame. Framing works because individuals are somewhat passive, and let their System 1 do the work. System 2 would need to be activated to validate whether the framing is correct. It needs attention. Importantly—and when the framing is connected with values attributes or perceptions—individuals tend to select options that are framed positively (as seen in the Asian disease example).

Second, in unknown and infrequent situations people have an *optimism bias,* which can reduce the perceived need for change. The availability heuristic does not work well when people are confronted with less familiar, infrequent decisions such as a large investment or an M&A deal. People who make such decisions frequently have a good sense of the risks involved, but those who don't tend to underestimate them. For example, when a market situation changes, as when a new technology is launched by a new market entrant and is endangering an incumbent player—a situation that does not occur very often in the life cycle of a firm—the managers of the incumbent firm tend to underweight the risks. They tend to look at the situation too optimistically and often delay necessary changes.

Third, people have a systematic *loss aversion bias.* Tests done many times with different people, of different cultures, have shown that the vast majority of people will not accept a bet that offers them a 50 percent probability of either winning $150 or losing $100. The pain of a loss is higher than the pleasure of a win. This means that people are unlikely to change a course of action if it implies losing the value of an investment that has already been made, even though the action may promise a higher outcome. The loss aversion bias produces inertia, the wish to stick to the current situation (Thaler and Sunstein 2008).

Fourth, people naturally tend to hold on to an existing position, which behavioral psychologists call the *status quo bias.* One of the causes of the status quo bias is lack of attention, and because people do not pay attention, they tend to settle for the default option offered to them (Thaler and Sunstein 2008). "If it works, don't change it," says our brain.

Addressing the Rigidities of Bounded Rationality

Understanding mental biases and heuristics—optimism, loss aversion, status-quo, and representativeness in particular—is particularly relevant when discussing organizational rigidities that hinder firms in reacting to changes in the environment. Why and how can they be addressed?

First, Dan Lovallo, a professor at the Australian School of Management, and Daniel Kahneman believe that companies can address the *optimism bias* by regularly bringing outside views and data into the organization (Lovallo and Kahneman 2003). Firms use different approaches to accomplish this goal. Some use the board of directors or a strategic advisory board as a source of information. Others use second opinions or critical challenges of plans and strategies by external industry experts. A large Swiss group is a good example of this approach. Every year, it invites four or five external challengers—external experts—to a two-day management workshop and asks them to shoot holes in the group's strategy. Not pleasant for the managers, but highly effective in bringing new insights and angles on a problem to the forefront. Another example is the way some private equity firms address the optimism bias by always taking a fresh look: After a partner has supervised a company for a few years, a different partner evaluates it anew (Lovallo and Sibony 2006).

Second, the *loss-aversion bias* may be reduced by making people less accountable for the losses caused by individual decisions (Beinhocker 2006). For example, managers can be evaluated on the basis of the performance of a portfolio of investments but not on losses on individual investments. The law of large numbers would then apply, and counterbalance the loss-aversion bias on individual investments.

Third, the *status quo bias* may be addressed by changing the default option. By making sure that the status quo is simply not among the available solutions, managers may get the members of the organization to move. Then, their response will be: "Yeah, I'll do whatever everybody else does."

Fourth, the *representativeness bias,* or mental model problem, may be addressed by fostering diversity in an organization. People with different experiences and different backgrounds tend to have different mental models, and they tend to see things differently. A diverse set of mental models in an organization increases the chance that at least one person will pick up, and correctly categorize, new information. Diversity works by getting a mix of different mental models into an organization.

Diversity, or at least mental flexibility in the workplace, can also be fostered at the individual level by promoting job rotation. It helps individuals to maintain flexibility and openness to new situations when they have worked in different functions within the firm (or, even better, within several firms). One extreme approach is to regularly rotate senior executives who run large organizational units. Sometimes, senior executives become less flexible, and over time they may tend to regard challenges to the organization they run as challenges or criticism of themselves. Otherwise highly capable executives, who nevertheless display excessively defensive and rigid behavior, and whose loss would be detrimental to the organization, may be helped by rotating them to run other large units of the firm.

It goes without saying that diversity of mental models only works in a culture of challenge and open debate.

■ ■ ■

Carl realized that the members of the GET were subject to *mental biases*. Furthermore, since they all shared similar experiences, they seemed to lack a sufficient diversity of *mental models*.

The six members had shared the same experience of believing the falsely rosy picture painted by the former CEO. Even though the GET members—and the board—now had up-to-date, concrete facts about AHD's problems, Carl was having a hard time getting them to confront the company's current reality. From John, who just wanted order in the ranks, to Arthur, who just wanted to make sure things got manufactured properly, the GET's members remained stuck in their own worlds—again, except Monica, the realist in finance.

Carl resolved to attack the issue forcefully.

He decided to massively increase the amount of market and competitive *information* available to the board and the GET. After examining his options, he took three actions:

1. He set up a strategy review process that intensively involved the board and his management team. Carl also organized things so that board and GET members would speak to at least three customers each, to hear directly about the quality problems they were facing, and about the better products and services offered by AHD's competitors.
2. Also, he asked three experienced individuals—all recently retired executives in similar industries—to independently challenge the strategies of the three business units run, in their own styles, by Sergei, Mark, and Luca.
3. Finally, Carl hired a reputable consultant, and assigned him to develop an in-depth market and competition analysis in all three of AHD's industry segments.

The process and the huge amount of new information it brought into AHD was eye-opening to most of the board members and the management team. It was clear to most of them that there was no room for optimism. AHD was struggling with quality problems in the orthopedics area. Very poor customer service in the diagnostics unit had led to AHD losing attractive contracts. Furthermore, AHD had missed important investment opportunities in new technologies in the diagnostics and dental units. Finally, AHD's expansion into emerging markets had flopped.

Even worse, outgrown by the key competitors, and having made hardly any money in the previous five years, AHD did not have the financial means to catch up quickly. It did not have the money to make a broad effort to simultaneously improve quality, invest in new technologies, and acquire firms in fast-growing emerging markets.

The analysis was eye-opening to most, but not to all, unfortunately. Two board members who had represented AHD's shareholders for almost two decades just couldn't see how bad the situation was.

One was Carlos, a retired medical doctor. He hadn't kept up to date with the latest technologies. Carl thought that—with three years until Carlos's retirement from the board—he was badly out of touch on matters such as patient needs and market dynamics. "He seemed to have switched off the engine a few years ago," Carl thought.

The other was Frank, a former professor in material sciences at the Massachusetts Institute of Technology. He was a co-inventor of the coating technology that had made AHD's implant products so successful in the early 1980s. Frank thought that, overall, AHD was doing fine. He had never believed in diversification, however, and thought that AHD should get rid of the diagnostics and dental businesses, and continue investing in and expanding the orthopedics business. Everyone else on the board understood that Frank was clearly caught in his *mental model.* But being stuck in an old mental model wasn't a problem for Frank alone.

Luca, the head of the diagnostics unit, was differently wired from most of the others on the management team. A loner, he did not engage during team discussions. Somewhat old-school and macho in manner, he wanted to run his own shop without what he saw as interference. He was concerned only about the diagnostics business, which—according to him and despite the quality issues—was doing well. In fact, it was not, but firmly set in his biases, he rejected any analysis or information that suggested the truth.

In the months that followed, Carl worked closely with Hubert to replace Carlos and Frank, with the aim of getting new and more relevant perspectives onto the board. They added Omar, an entrepreneur from the Middle East who knew many of the fast-growing markets well, and Phillip, a

Dutch professor, who was teaching genomics at the University of Antwerp, and who would bring the latest insights on genomics into the board, since genomics were revolutionizing the diagnostics market.

Then Carl spoke to Luca and gently but firmly told him it was time for him to retire from AHD. The discussion was difficult, but it was necessary. Luca was very angry to start with, but—once it was clear that the decision was final—he accepted it and moved on quickly. Within a few weeks, he had a job with a pharmaceutical manufacturer outside New York.

Carl asked Mark to take over the diagnostics business. Mark was a thoughtful, inspirational, and collaborative leader, and Carl thought that he would bring new ideas and a great deal of energy to the diagnostics business. At the same time, Carl believed that a fresh (and less defensive) view would also do no harm to the orthopedics unit, which Mark had been leading for nearly seven years. Being detached from his turf was wrenching for Mark, but given the obvious respect Carl had for his leadership abilities, he gradually made the adjustment. And, perhaps, he had come to understand that his protective stance about the orthopedic unit was holding him back.

With John's somewhat reluctant concurrence, Carl reached into the U.S. regional organization and promoted Mike, the head of the Americas Commercial division, to run the orthopedics unit.

Mike, a calm, fit Oregonian with an Ivy League MBA, was convivial and innovative, marrying the pioneer attitude of the western United States with a solid business background. Having spent years out in the field—competently holding focused business meetings across the United States, often followed by equally competent and focused rounds of golf or tennis—he knew AHD's major customers on a personal basis and understood their needs better than anyone else at AHD. In particular, he knew what it took to win in the U.S. market, where AHD's orthopedics products still did not have a strong position.

Mike looked to Mark to bring him up to speed on the orthopedics division, but he felt comfortable as a leader and, despite a tendency to be more casual than some of his peers, Mike added to the GET's collegiality. Sergei was somewhat surprised by his manner, but Monica actually unbent enough to have a glass of wine with Mike—he had a beer—after she and her top accountants had spent a day with him reviewing the orthopedic figures.

Two of AHD's business units, orthopedics and diagnostics, now had new leaders.

With a renewed board and a renewed, better aligned management team, AHD started developing measures to make up for the time lost in the previous five years. As the company lacked the money and the critical mass—but not the skills—to simultaneously improve quality and expand into new technologies and new markets, the board and the GET decided to pursue an aggressive strategy, which they called an open architecture strategy, to gain access to new technologies and services.

Instead of doing everything by itself, a hallmark of the GET's previous approach, AHD would aggressively exploit the strengths of its strategic partners. These partners would complement AHD's product offerings where they were weak. AHD had world-class orthopedics implants, dental implants, and diagnostics products, but many of its complementary products (such as consumables) and the services that made up part of its offering to clinics and hospitals were not competitive. The industry thus generally regarded AHD's overall offerings as noncompetitive, or at least less competitive than others on the market.

The board and the management team decided to discontinue investments in complementary products and services, and source them from strategic partners instead.

But the open architecture approach went beyond products. The board agreed to the GET's proposals for a number of joint ventures to get quick access to new technologies to further new developments in the orthopedics, dental, and diagnostics product lines. Lastly, the board agreed on an expansion strategy that would make use of joint ventures with local producers and distributors in fast-growing emerging markets.

Successful implementation of this strategy would create significant wealth for the company's managers and employees alike, at least according to Monica's calculations.

Carl was visibly satisfied. The board and the management team shared a common understanding of the challenges that AHD was facing. And they had agreed on a strategy—building on a modern and effective open architecture approach in product offering, research and development, and geographic expansion—that would allow them to catch up with their competitors and regain a leading position in the industry, and all this with minimal capital investment.

Carl communicated the new strategy to all of AHD's employees with a series of town hall–like meetings and broadcasts at which he also answered questions, to get his people as engaged as possible. And he gave interviews that were posted on the company intranet. To facilitate communication, the new strategy was branded the OPEN strategy.

At first, things seemed to be going quite well. However, over the months that followed, Carl's mood changed.

The OPEN strategy didn't seem to be working. Though it had worked very well with KenkoInc in Asia, the open architecture strategy did not seem to suit AHD's customer base.

Customers didn't seem to care much for offerings based on an open architecture approach. Oddly, while the customers—mostly clinics and hospitals—used to buy a large part of AHD's entire old product range, they seemed to change their purchasing behavior when they were offered solutions based on an open architecture approach, combining best-of-breed products and services from different companies. The first reaction was that customers were themselves well equipped to buy the best products and services from the best suppliers. AHD's proposition of bundling best-of-breed solutions didn't seem convincing to them. Oddly, AHD was selling less instead of more with the new approach.

Carl speculated that the source of the problem was that AHD's sales force hadn't really bought into the concept. Sales reps didn't seem to feel comfortable selling products and services from other companies in tandem with AHD's offerings. As a consequence, the commercial organization wasn't approaching customers in a convincing manner. He speculated that the sales training hadn't been sufficient, and that he would need to change that. Also, some of the product teams weren't really supporting the OPEN approach, and were preventing their products from working seamlessly together with products and services sourced from external partners. At first, Carl thought that these issues could be easily fixed.

But an increasing number of people in the board and the GET started to question the validity of the strategy. Many felt that AHD did not have the capabilities, in the sales force or in product management, or in the rest of the firm, to implement the new strategy. There was no tradition of working with strategic partners in joint ventures, in product management, in sales, or in emerging markets.

"The strategy works on paper, but not in practice," he remembered Fred, a board member, saying. Fred was a dour senior manager at a firm of auditors. "What the hell does this guy know about what works in practice? All Fred does is produce paper!" Carl thought.

The matter escalated into a vivid and animated discussion within the board. The majority of the board believed that AHD should go back to its old strategy. After all, it had worked for some time in the past. It had served AHD well, some said. Maybe a renewed effort could be made to make the old strategy work. Maybe all it needed was greater efforts to improve the complementary products that hadn't been the most competitive in the past five years or so.

Some board members thought that the only matter that needed attention was AHD's poor profitability. They suggested launching a cost-cutting program. Needless to say, Fred, the auditor, was part of this group.

Another group, led by Martin, a former investment banker who was pompous and cautious in equal measure, made a best-owner argument. "AHD should just get rid of the orthopedics business," he proclaimed. "It's had the biggest loss of market share in the past five years. AHD is not the best owner."

Some of the most outspoken members of Martin's group thought that AHD should even investigate a full merger-of-equals with DMT. The merger of equals idea sounded good but it was clear to Carl—and, separately, to Hubert as well—that this solution would have implied a de facto takeover of AHD by DMT.

In Carl's presence, the board decided to vote on the question of whether the new strategy should be discontinued.

The vote in the board was split, five to five. The new members, Omar and Frank, backed Carl. Hubert, the senior director, did so, too, but his intentions were clear. He spoke for the whole of the board when he said, "You have three months to make this OPEN strategy work. If it fails, we'll look for a new strategy, including the possibility of selling some of the company—or all of it."

After this announcement from his firmest supporter, Carl was deeply frustrated and somewhat alarmed. He could not understand why—after only a few months—the board and the GET team would discard a strategy that they had jointly developed, and that everybody felt was viable. He had been head of the company only nine months. A three-month window would mark the end of his first year at AHD. It seemed that given customers' initial lukewarm reaction to the new strategy, his board and his executive team were already giving up.

How could it be that, after the first adverse reactions, people were already raising doubts about AHD's ability to implement the new strategy? Why were they not more persevering? Why were they ready to surrender so quickly? Carl couldn't help but worry that if the board sold the company after he had put in only a year as CEO, his executive career would suffer for years.

A week or so later, Carl was on a flight to Zurich for an operating review with the European region. He sat next to a soft-spoken older gentleman. They started chatting and exchanging views on contemporary matters. The man was interesting and clearly well educated. He was of Polish origin and had left his native country as a young child shortly after the Second World

War. He had studied in the United States and made a career in science. He was a distinguished professor of psychology at one of the elite U.S. universities. They spoke about many matters, but the conversation took an interesting turn when they discussed the professor's research into human self-confidence and perseverance.

It would turn out to be a very illuminating conversation.

CHAPTER 4

The Greatest of All Time

Roger was crying. It was a very emotional moment witnessed by 15,000 people in the Rod Laver Arena at Melbourne Park in Melbourne, Australia, and by millions of TV spectators worldwide. In late January 2009, on a warm Australian summer evening, Roger Federer had just lost the Australian Open final to Rafael Nadal, his long-time opponent. Roger had come to Australia to equalize Pete Sampras's record of 14 Grand Slam titles. He had failed, and nobody at that moment believed that he would ever win a major title again.

He would never return to being the world's number one tennis player, a title he had held for many years. Sampras would remain the undisputed greatest of all time in professional tennis. For the press and the tennis experts around the world, one thing was clear: The Federer era was over.

In the months that followed, Federer did not win one single major tournament. He lost mostly to players against whom he had seemed unbeatable only one year before. His career seemed to be spiraling downward.

But not to one person: not to Roger himself. Every time he was interviewed, he would repeat: His objective was to again become the world's best tennis player and to beat Sampras's record of Grand Slam titles. Many interpreted his remarks as denial that his time as the world's best had passed. He trained and worked hard, convinced that he could make it. Later that year, he won the French and the U.S. Opens, and in January 2010, he was back at Melbourne Park, lifting the trophy. With 16 Grand Slam titles, Federer was now tennis's GOAT, the Greatest of All Time.

There are many GOATs in business, leaders who endured many setbacks and persevered against great odds.

For example, in the early phase of its development, and to enhance its chances of securing funding, Bell Telephone offered all its rights to Western Union for $100,000. Western Union refused, saying, "What use could this company make of an electrical toy?" (Bandura 1997)

There are also examples from the arts. Van Gogh sold only one painting during his life, and Rodin was rejected three times by the École des Beaux Arts in Paris. The Beatles were turned down by several record companies. Decca Records rejected them on the grounds that "We don't like their music. Groups of guitars are [...] out." Many of the literary classics brought their authors innumerable rejections. James Joyce's *Dubliners* was rejected by 22 publishers. The novelist William Saroyan received more than 1,000 rejections before his first piece was published (Bandura 1997).

It seems that sometimes the path to success is paved with difficulties, but eventual winners are resilient and persevere against great odds. Thomas Edison, who changed the world with many crucial inventions, such as the phonograph, the light bulb, and the motion picture camera, once said: "The trouble with the other inventors is that they try a few things and quit. I never quit until I get what I want" (Bandura 1997). Interestingly, it is people like Thomas Edison who help organizations to adapt and succeed.

After mental biases and heuristics, lack of perseverance is the second individual rigidity, or why individuals and, ultimately, firms sometimes fail to adapt and to respond to challenges. To better understand how the minds of those who really persevere in the face of apparently insurmountable obstacles work, we need to dive into psychology and look at the theory of self-efficacy beliefs.

The Theory of Self-Efficacy Beliefs

In the 1960s, Albert Bandura, a Canadian psychologist, was working with snake-phobic patients. He wanted to help them master their fears. In the course of his work, Bandura found that task-specific self-confidence—which he called self-efficacy beliefs—improved the ability to cope with and adapt to unpleasant situations, and reduced fear in his patients.

Bandura spent a significant part of his career exploring the role that self-efficacy beliefs play in human functioning. In 1977, Bandura published *Social Learning Theory,* a book that changed research in psychology in the 1980s (Bandura 1977).

Today, he is the David Starr Jordan Professor Emeritus of Social Science in Psychology at Stanford University. A survey in 2002 named Bandura as the fourth most frequently cited psychologist of all time, behind B. F. Skinner, Sigmund Freud, and Jean Piaget, and as the most cited living one (Haggbloom 2002). He is widely regarded as one of the most influential psychologists alive.

Bandura defined belief of self-efficacy as a personal judgment of "how well one can execute courses of action required to deal with prospective situations" (Bandura 1982).

People who doubt their capabilities, who lack self-confidence in specific domains of activity shy away from difficult tasks in those domains. They have low aspirations and weak focus and commitment to the goals that they chose to pursue. In difficult and taxing situations, they dwell on their personal deficiencies, the formidable nature of the task, and the adverse consequences of failure. Such thinking undermines their efforts. It diverts attention from how to best execute activities to concerns over personal deficiencies. They are also slow to recover from failures or setbacks. Because they are prone to diagnose poor or insufficient performance as deficient aptitude, it does not require much failure for them to lose faith in their capabilities (Bandura 1997).

In contrast, people who have strong beliefs of self-efficacy approach difficult tasks as challenges to be mastered rather than threats to be avoided. They set themselves demanding goals and maintain strong focus and commitment to them. People with healthy self-confidence invest a high level of effort in what they do and maintain or even heighten their effort in the face of failure or setbacks. They attribute failure to insufficient effort, not to aptitude. They remain task-focused and committed (Bandura 1997).

In his classic *Self-Efficacy: The Exercise of Control,* Bandura uses numerous studies and examples to illustrate the theory of self-efficacy. For example, he cites an experiment in which children who perceived themselves to be high in mathematical efficacy were more successful in solving mathematical problems than were children who doubted their own skills (even though they had the same mathematical skill level). He also cites a study that shows that schools in which the members of the staff have a strong sense of collective efficacy flourish academically. In contrast, schools in which the staffers have doubts about their academic efficacy decline academically (Bandura 1997).

It is important to distinguish belief of self-efficacy from a generally well-developed and rounded personality, or general self-confidence. Perceptions of ability should not be seen as traits that govern the entire personality

(Bandura 1997). People can be very insecure intimately and have one complex or another, yet they may hold the belief that they are efficacious at a specific task or activity. A person, say a molecular biologist, can be an insecure person, with complexes, yet believe she is the best in that profession.

Also, and perhaps most importantly, the belief of self-efficacy is an incremental skill that can be acquired and developed over time. In practice, unfortunately, self-efficacy is often perceived as an individual's given strength, an inherent aptitude, or endowed capability. Sometimes, individuals in organizations are perceived by others as being insecure, defensive of their own work, and inflexible in adapting to new situations and in addressing new challenges. Such individuals are often removed from their positions, even if this implies a loss to the organization in terms of specific experience, relationships, or technical capabilities and skills.

Understanding how and when to invest in developing individuals' self-efficacy beliefs helps leaders to develop a more nuanced perspective on when to remove or when to build on particular individuals in key positions and key roles in the organization.

Developing self-confidence takes time. The decision whether to remove an individual lacking self-confidence from a position is therefore, among other considerations, a trade-off between the time it takes to develop self-efficacy beliefs versus the time it takes to create experience, relationships, and technical skills, which may be lost when an individual is removed from his position in an organization.

Recent research suggests that the concept of self-efficacy can be extended to groups and organizations. Resistance to change by groups of people or organizations, or rather an inability to adapt, may be caused by low collective self-efficacy expectations. If teams or organizations do not believe that they can successfully solve a new problem or face an unfamiliar situation, they probably will not succeed (Gist 1987; Stajkovic, Lee, and Nyberg 2009).

A Positive for Organizations

A number of studies have demonstrated the positive relationship between belief of self-efficacy and behavioral effectiveness in organizational settings, in areas such as adaptability to advanced technology, managerial idea generation, and learning (Gist 1987; Stajkovic and Luthans 1998; Sadri and Robertson 1993).

In a study published in 1998, Alexander Stajkovic of the University of California and Fred Luthans of the University of Nebraska summarized the research findings pertaining to the relationship between task-specific self-confidence and work-related performance.

They found a strong positive correlation between belief of self-efficacy and work-related performance. A glimpse of the blindingly obvious, one might think. Yet what was surprising was the magnitude of the impact of increased perception of self-efficacy on performance and, relative to other interventions, to boost performance.

They compared interventions to increase the belief of self-efficacy of organization members with three other types of work-related interventions: goal setting, feedback, and organizational behavior modification programs.

Motivation to increase performance through goal setting is one of the most researched areas of work-related behavior in psychology. Evidence from numerous field studies and experiments shows that setting explicit, challenging goals significantly enhances motivation and work-related performance (Bandura 1997). Goals have more impact when combined with feedback, and even more so when combined with selected training to close performance gaps (which Stajkovic and Luthans call an organizational behavior modification program).

Stajkovic and Luthans have shown that interventions to increase self-efficacy achieve significantly more impact than the other three types of interventions (Figure 4.1).

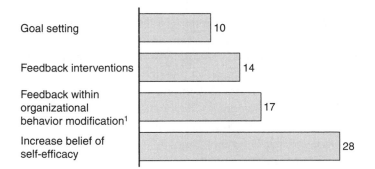

FIGURE 4.1   Improvement in Performance with Selected Interventions (in percent)

[1]The organizational behavior modification program is a formal systematic method for setting behavioral expectations, measuring the results, and intervening to close gaps.
Data source: Stajkovic, A. D., and F. Luthans. "Self-Efficacy and Work-Related Performance: A Meta-Analysis." *Psychological Bulletin* 124, no. 2: 240–261.

Pathways of Self-Confidence

The reason for the impressive impact of increasing the belief of self-efficacy stems from understanding that self-efficacy works through four major processes to affect performance. They are cognitive, motivational, affective, and selective processes (Bandura 1997).

Efficacy beliefs affect *cognitive processes,* thought patterns that can improve work-related adaptation and performance. In a program of research on complex decision making at the end of the 1980s, Wood and Bandura showed that strong beliefs of self-efficacy lead people to improve in two ways. First, people set themselves higher and more ambitious goals. Second, people make more efficient use of analytical strategies and better use of problem-solving techniques. Among students with the same level of ability but differing senses of efficacy, those with a stronger sense of efficacy are quicker to discard faulty cognitive strategies and less inclined to reject good solutions prematurely (Wood and Bandura 1989). They seem to apply more rational problem-solving techniques, and they are less likely to fall victim to the mental biases that we discussed in the previous chapter.

Efficacy beliefs affect *motivational processes,* too. First, as we discussed earlier, goals *per se* improve performance, and people with a strong belief of self-efficacy tend to set higher goals for themselves. Second, people also motivate themselves by the outcome (for example, nonmonetary or monetary incentives) that they expect from their behavior. People with a strong sense of self-efficacy assign a higher probability of success to achieving a given outcome. In other words, the expected value of an outcome is higher with people who have a strong sense of efficacy (what psychologists call expectancy value theory).

Efficacy beliefs also affect *emotional processes.* We will see in the next chapter that novel situations, such as a change of strategy or a competitive threat, create anxiety and inhibit learning and adaptation by individuals (and eventually by organizations). Efficacy beliefs help people control their emotions better in the face of novel situations. Efficacy beliefs strengthen a sense of control and self-determination, and can help individuals keep their (negative) emotions under control.

The first three processes—cognitive, motivational, and emotional—enable people to function better and exercise better control over their emotions in a given situation. Self-efficacy also affects performance through a *selection process,* in that people also select the situation in which they are more likely to perform. In selecting possible courses of action, people tend to avoid situations that they believe exceed their capabilities, but pick situations that they judge themselves capable of handling. Career choices are an example of this. People who believe that they are good at mathematics are more likely to join an accounting firm than a creative firm. This selection factor also has implications for adaptation by firms. Management teams will only consider strategies that match their perceived (but not necessarily existing) skills and capabilities, and so limit the solution space of their strategy.

Developing Self-Efficacy

The three most effective approaches to developing a strong belief of self-efficacy in individuals are enactive mastery, vicarious experience, and verbal persuasion (Gist 1987).

First, and most effective, is *enactive mastery,* defined as repeated performance accomplishment (achieving goals and learning by doing). Mastery is facilitated when gradual accomplishments build the skills and abilities needed to perform a given activity. Leaders should set goals that are perceived by those whom they lead as ambitious but achievable. Achieving such goals builds confidence and gradually gets people to set more ambitious goals for themselves. In contrast, by setting unrealistic targets, a leader risks reducing the engagement of the people she leads and lowering their self-confidence.

Second, the next most effective is *vicarious experience,* that is, learning from *role models.* This is most effective when people can relate to the role models (similar background, age, and so on), and when role models succeed after overcoming difficulties, rather than when they achieve success easily. Role models who succeed in seemingly difficult and challenging situations are inspiring, produce followership, and cause followers to copy their behavior, and—if they are successful—to achieve enactive mastery.

Third is *verbal persuasion,* which is aimed at convincing a person of his ability to perform a specific activity ("Yes, you can do it!"). Verbal persuasion is, however, believed to be less effective than enactive mastery or role modeling.

A Health Warning

Sometimes, the perceived self-efficacy of individuals or groups can be too high, producing excessive optimism, overconfidence, and potentially misguided behavior.

In his book *How the Mighty Fall,* Jim Collins describes and analyzes the fall of once-great firms. He believes that one of the seeds of decline lies in management teams becoming insulated by success. People become arrogant, they fail to acknowledge the very reasons for their success, and they overestimate their own merits and capabilities (Collins 2009).

Such a situation is believed to have occurred among the members of President John F. Kennedy's inner circle, and to have led to the fiasco in Vietnam. Arthur Schlesinger, a U.S. historian and assistant to President Kennedy from 1961 to 1963, wrote a detailed account of the Kennedy Administration, titled *A Thousand Days* (Schlesinger 1965).

He was quoted as saying, "Euphoria reigned. We thought for a moment that the world was plastic and the future unlimited" (Gist 1987). The source of the exaggerated belief of self-efficacy may have been grounded in President Kennedy's own enacted mastery and his emergence and election as president against all the odds. While his success certainly should have generated a strong sense of self-efficacy, it may have also led to overconfidence and a sense of infallibility among his aides.

As much as they foster self-efficacy, leaders also need to be careful to avoid overoptimism and arrogance, and work to moderate self-efficacy.

The CEO of a large firm once explained to me that whenever one of his senior managers is too self-critical and too concerned about the future, he encourages him to think about his strengths, and to think about more possibilities and opportunities to shape the future favorably. But whenever the senior manager gets ahead of himself, becoming too optimistic, he warns him and reminds him of the limitations and dangers ahead. This is an excellent example of managing self-efficacy beliefs in practice.

Implications for Management

If used carefully, fostering self-confidence can be a very powerful tool to increase the ability of individuals (and organizations) to adapt to changing situations.

This has five implications for management: on staffing of key positions with learners, on target setting, on performance appraisal practices, on leadership development, and on training practices.

Staffing Key Positions with Learners

It is obvious that key positions, positions that are important for the achievement of results and for adaptation, need to be staffed with people with a healthy sense of self-efficacy. Some organizational areas or departments—such as research and development, marketing, or technology—may be more important for adaptation than others. Undoubtedly, the top team is one of these areas.

The organization's leader does not always have a perfect team, however, and her freedom to make changes may be limited by a lack of alternatives, by fear of the loss of specific knowledge, or by the fact that she has previously made commitments to specific people.

It may be important to assess members of the top team not only on their existing capabilities and their existing belief of self-efficacy, but also on their flexibility and attitude toward learning. With a bit of support and positive framing, they may have the ability to develop a healthy level of self-confidence (as exemplified by the case of Sergei, the head of AHD's dental implant unit, later in this chapter).

Several studies have shown that individuals who have a positive attitude toward learning, people who regard self-efficacy as an *acquirable skill,* tend to seek challenges that provide opportunities to expand their knowledge and capabilities. They regard errors as a natural part of the learning process and view setbacks not as personal failures but as learning experiences.

By contrast, people who view ability as an *inherent aptitude,* an endowment, seek tasks that minimize the probability of failure. They are more rigid, and often become defensive when their work is challenged, as setbacks or negatively perceived feedback represent threats and reveal their limitations. They set themselves unambitious goals, and they shun opportunities to learn more (Bandura 1997).

In a study by Wood and Bandura, the quality of decision making by managers who view their decision-making ability as reflecting inherent cognitive aptitude deteriorated when they encountered problems. They started setting themselves lower targets, their problem solving became more erratic, and in consequence they achieved progressively less with the organizations they were managing. By contrast, with managers who believed that efficacy is an acquirable skill, the quality of decision making increased, as did the performance of the organization they were managing (Figure 4.2, Wood and Bandura 1989).

One more subtle implication is that firms may need to embed learning and learning aptitude as values or norms in the corporate culture. We discuss this point later.

Target Setting

As seen earlier, the achievement of ambitious goals builds confidence and gets people to set even higher goals for themselves. The implication is that

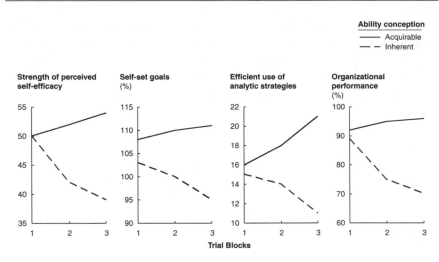

FIGURE 4.2   **Performance Development under Instilled Conceptions of Ability**

Source: Self-Efficacy: The Exercise of Self-Control by Albert Bandura. © 1997 by W. H. Freeman and Company. Used with permission of Worth Publishers.

leaders need to be very thoughtful in setting targets. Targets should ideally be ambitious so they can better foster motivation, innovative thinking, and problem solving, but they should be still realistic and achievable.

Clearly unachievable targets lead to loss of confidence, or at best to lack of engagement and commitment by those who receive those targets ("these are not my numbers," "not my goals").

Performance Appraisal Practices

As seen in this chapter, positive achievements support the development of self-efficacy. However, many firms have practices built into their performance appraisal systems that foster a low sense of efficacy.

Some firms sort their employees into ability groups (so-called forced rankings, typically with a normal distribution of some low performers, many on-track performers, and very few high performers), which diminishes the perceived self-efficacy of those in lower rating categories. Competitive grading practices convert performance evaluations into experiences in which many are doomed to failure for the success of a very few (Bandura 1997).

On the other hand, individualized performance feedback—in which the ratings are relative to individual achievements (deviation from budget, degree of individual target achievement, for example)—may be more powerful in developing a more self-confident, adaptive, high performance corporate environment.

Leadership Development

Leadership plays a key role in the development of self-efficacy. The implication is that all leaders—from senior executives, middle managers, and department heads to front-line leaders—may need to receive the appropriate training to foster self-efficacy beliefs in the people they lead. This includes developing the ability to judge the strengths and weaknesses of their subordinates, and their attitude to learning, and then to select the approach best suited to enhance their sense of self-confidence—such as enacting mastery, purposeful role modeling, verbal persuasion, or selecting a job better suited to them.

Training Practices

Self-efficacy theory has been applied successfully in the redesign of the training curricula of many firms. In essence, the application of self-efficacy theory leads to *mastery modeling* or *forum and field training approaches,* which include three main elements. First, the skills to be taught are modeled by trainers in a class setting to convey the basic rules and problem-solving strategies. Second, the learners carry out guided practice under simulated conditions. Third, the learners apply their newly learned skills in their work situation. In essence, this means breaking down the formal teaching into chunks, with time in between for the learners to reflect, experiment, and apply the new principles (Lawson and Price 2003).

Success Built to Last co-author Jerry Porras (Porras, Emery, and Thompson 2007), the Emeritus Lane Professor of Organizational Behavior and Change at Stanford University, and his colleagues demonstrated that supervisory skills instilled with a mastery-modeling approach significantly improve the morale and the productivity of organizations (Porras and Anderson 1981; Porras et al. 1982). They showed that this approach improved the level of monthly productivity of a manufacturing plant by 17 percent while significantly decreasing absenteeism and employee turnover.

■ ■ ■

Carl came to see that the issue with the board and the GET was not a matter of a lack of understanding. It was clear to the majority of the board and the GET team that the market had become tougher and that AHD had to change its strategy. The issue was a lack of individual and collective *self-confidence*. And Carl had to fix it fast, before they sold the company out from under him.

As soon as the first setbacks and difficulties with the OPEN strategy became apparent, some members of the GET were quick to share their skepticism about it. Sergei, head of dental implants, was the most vocal.

Sergei had been instrumental in building the dental unit in the 1990s. He knew the industry and its customers better than anyone else, and he had good business acumen. Though highly analytical and somewhat mechanistic in his thinking, he was a very astute people leader. He could at times be quite irritable and impulsive, but he was also charming and warm-hearted, and enjoyed an excellent following within his division. In regard to self-efficacy, though, Sergei was very insecure and defensive. He made it clear several times that he perceived the entire discussion about a possible change of strategy as an attack on his work and on his person. He rejected the need for change, particularly in his own division.

"We're doing fine," he protested to Carl, "you just don't trust my team, or me."

"Actually," Carl said to him, "that's not the case at all. We're not doing that well, but I have more confidence in you than you do."

Given Sergei's acumen, experience, and strong leadership skills, Carl wanted to keep him on board, so he began to invest a lot of time in one-on-one discussions, some in the office, some over lunches at a series of restaurants where Sergei's sophisticated knowledge of cuisine led them to share some excellent meals. Most of the time, Carl asked questions: "What are your concerns, Sergei?" "Why do you say that?" "What could we do differently?" He spent most of the discussions listening.

Carl came to see that having lost his former boss and having to cope with a new one made Sergei anxious and insecure. Sergei often talked about Rittenhouse, about their relationship, about the support he had enjoyed. Sergei had been one of Rittenhouse's favorite management team members and had his full trust and confidence. On the other hand, Sergei was not at all sure yet about Carl's intentions. Being Sergei, he generally assumed the worst. He often spoke of "we" (himself and Rittenhouse) when describing AHD's achievements in building the dental implant business, though it was very clear to Carl—who by now knew a good bit more than Sergei did about his predecessor's shortcomings—that Sergei had been the unit's true architect and builder.

Convinced of Sergei's ability, Carl wrapped up one of their discussions with an invitation. "Sergei," he said, "I want you to lead an important part of the OPEN strategy's implementation: training the sales force. This is crucial for us, and I think you know how to make it work."

Given such a strong, visible sign of Carl's confidence and trust, Sergei agreed. When Carl backed up these new assignments with many smaller gestures and instances of positive reinforcement, like increasing Sergei's staff and budget to accommodate his new training responsibilities, the moves had the impact Carl had hoped to achieve. As Sergei's self-confidence and openness to challenges grew, so did Carl's conviction that he would become a stronger—more flexible and less defensive—member of AHD's top team.

Sergei's new training assignment went well, and his dental implant division continued to regain strength, so Carl soon came to him with an additional assignment: to help him engage the GET and the board in discussing ways to implement OPEN, not ways to kill it. "I need full buy-in," Carl told Sergei, "and you're the one who can help me get it."

When Sergei answered confidently, "I think we can do that together," Carl knew he had won at least one battle. But he still had a war to fight: The board and the GET collectively lacked self-confidence and most of AHD's top leaders were ready to give up on the new OPEN strategy.

Carl knew he could reiterate the rationale for change and the need for the new strategy to the board and the management team, and he could explain how AHD would implement it, but it was clear that persuasion would not be enough.

Carl had to *role model* the new strategy, hoping that he would succeed, and hoping that eventually others in the organization would follow him, given the known power of vicarious experience.

He decided that he would try to demonstrate the new approach by winning back a particularly difficult customer from the competition. He chose the Meyer Hospital Group, which had been an important European customer for almost a decade in the past. However, a few years earlier, Meyer Hospital Group—which had grown tired of AHD's lack of responsiveness and the declining quality of its products—had given its business to the Devica Group, a local medical device firm.

Carl asked for a meeting with Meyer Hospital Group's CEO, a young but admired leader in the German business community, who took a while to respond. When they finally met, Carl explained AHD's new strategy and approach, and asked for a chance to work with Meyer Hospital Group again.

Meyer Hospital Group's CEO wasn't at all interested in working with AHD; quite the opposite. He spent almost an hour complaining to Carl about AHD.

"The company gradually got very arrogant," the CEO protested. "Your people stopped listening to us and neglected our needs—we ran out of supplies; we received short orders and shoddy merchandise. We could never get the right people to pay attention. The whole situation was deteriorating—and we got the sense that nobody at AHD cared at all."

Carl tried to explain that a new day had dawned at AHD, but it wasn't a good meeting. He felt close to defeat when he left. "Maybe the board and the GET were right to question my strategy," he thought morosely on the way home.

The next evening he was back home in New Jersey. After the children went to bed, Carl talked to Gwen and recounted his tough meeting. She already knew all about the doubts that the board and the top team had voiced, and the ultimatum they had issued. Carl sighed, "Maybe I'm wrong this time. It sure is turning out to be an uphill climb."

"Stick with it," Gwen suggested. "I don't suppose it's going to be easy, but I do think you're going to get there."

"I'm giving it my best shot," Carl said, "but I've got only six weeks left before they could put a for-sale sign on the whole company."

A week later, Carl got a call from Meyer's CEO.

"I have something for you. It is small, and it is going to be a competitive bidding process, but I want to give you a chance. We have a clinic in Southern Bavaria, and we want a bid on modernizing our diagnostic center. Can you do it?" he asked.

"We will do our best," Carl said, and the CEO knew he meant it.

The next day Carl went to Hubert to tell him about Sergei's successful sales training campaign and the request for a proposal. Heartened, but not yet persuaded, Hubert made a couple of phone calls to other directors and gave Carl three more months to prove his case.

Carl would survive his first anniversary as AHD's CEO—making it to the second one was up to him.

Carl gathered the best team AHD could put together and flew with the team members to meet the busy chief physician heading the small clinic in Southern Bavaria. Carl knew AHD had to completely understand the clinic's needs and requirements. The AHD team worked for three weeks, literally day and night, to design an end-to-end, open-architecture solution that would ideally fit the clinic's needs. They worked closely and intensively with their strategic partners to develop the offering to outfit the new small diagnostic center. Then they submitted their bid.

Carl soon got a call from the head of Meyer. "Okay," he said, "you're on. Show me what you can do, you and your supposedly new AHD."

Two months later, the new diagnostic center was up and running. It was the best diagnostic center AHD had ever built, and it was a success. The chief physician beamed as he led Meyer Hospital Group and AHD executives on a tour of the new facility.

Before long, Carl was asked to refit all of Meyer Hospital Group's diagnostic centers. It was a huge request, but this time it was not a competitive bid. AHD had the job. Clearly, it had regained Meyer Hospital Group's confidence. A tough thing to do, but AHD had succeeded.

The Meyer Hospital Group story boosted the morale of AHD's employees—but more importantly, it gave the OPEN strategy enormous credibility at the top of the company. The board took a vote on it again, and this time supported it unanimously. Not only did the board now understand the new strategy—thanks to this success and Sergei's successful behind-the-scenes lobbying—the members also saw that it worked in practice. And so did the GET. The way AHD and its strategic partners had developed and captured this opportunity inspired the organization and created followership, especially among AHD's top 100 or so executives.

Carl wanted to capitalize on the moment and accelerate the adoption of the new OPEN strategy. Beyond broadcasting the Meyer Hospital Group story widely within the organization, he introduced an "OPEN Award" to be given to key account management teams that won contracts with innovative, open architecture–based solutions.

In the months that followed, though, Carl began to worry that AHD's change was only skin deep. While the Meyer Hospital Group story had created enthusiasm, many pivotal customer teams—known as key account teams—did not change their behavior very much. They called their solutions "OPEN," but in fact they were largely selling their customers core product offerings with complementary products that were mostly produced internally. They were sticking to AHD's old approach—only the title was new.

In fact, everybody in AHD was now using the OPEN brand. With the aim of exploiting the successful OPEN story (and to increase acceptance in AHD's organization), almost everything that had to appear modern and innovative was now called OPEN. There was an OPEN sales process, an OPEN finance model, and an OPEN supply chain approach. The way this was taken to extreme lengths ultimately devalued the concept. Without deliberate irony, the information technology department even launched a new OPEN VPN system (a *virtual private network,* a closed user-group communication network).

But despite the OPEN brand, the solutions AHD was selling to its customers were still largely based only on internally developed products and services. It seemed that when it came to really changing the offerings, and sourcing the best products and services from strategic partners—whether for refitting a diagnostic center or an orthopedics operating room—most of the sales reps continued to offer the old trusted (but not very successful) solutions.

Carl was puzzled. The organization understood the need for change. Everybody had seen the new OPEN strategy work with Meyer Hospital Group. The company offered employees clear incentives to adopt the new strategy. Sergei had trained the salespeople extensively. There was even an OPEN Award. Yet when it came to actually changing behavior, not much was happening.

It was frustrating, and Carl couldn't understand why people were clinging to their old habits as if they were on autopilot.

That Friday night, a warm evening in the early summer of 2006, Gwen and Carl had friends to dinner: Ernest and Lucie, and Andrew and Franca. Ernest was a successful private banker, while Lucie was a neuroscientist at Boston University, researching brain functions in reptiles and small mammals (mainly mice). Franca was a pediatrician, and Andrew was a heart surgeon, who came to dinner feeling somewhat down because James, one of his most likable patients, had died that week.

Andrew had performed a bypass for James a year earlier and had strongly advised him to lose weight and change his diet. After a pretty good start on his new regimen, James had returned to his old habits. That Monday, he'd suffered a heart attack and died suddenly.

It wasn't a great conversation at first, but it took an interesting turn when Gwen asked: "Why do people like James, who know that they have to change their behavior, resist change even if doing so will almost certainly lead to death? We know people do behave like this, but *why,* Carl?" Once again, Gwen had given Carl food for thought.

CHAPTER 5

Rewiring Brains

Lack of patient compliance with doctors' prescriptions is a big issue in medicine.

Up to 50 percent of diagnosed hypertension patients fail to take their medication regularly and remain uncontrolled, despite the significant long-term risks.

Even worse, 90 percent of people who have had coronary bypasses do not change their unhealthy lifestyles, even though they are fully aware of the risks they run. They know that they need to exercise and to lose weight, and that otherwise they may suffer a stroke or another cardiac incident, and yet they don't follow through.

But the matter goes beyond compliance with medical prescriptions. Most of us want to lose weight. We want to look and feel fit. We want to exercise and change our diet. I start a new diet every Monday morning. By Tuesday I usually succumb to the sweets in the kitchen, and I say to myself: "I'll start next week."

W hy don't people who know that their behavior isn't right make the changes they need, even when changing is clearly and unambiguously in their best interests, and if it comes at a low cost (such as taking a pill or exercising)?

In the past two chapters we dove into psychology and studied thinking biases and heuristics and the concept of self-efficacy and the behaviors they produce. In this chapter—and with the help of cognitive neuroscience—we dive deeper into the brain and into the concept of neuroplasticity to understand what it takes to change our behaviors and our habits. Lack of behavioral change is the third and last factor of individual rigidity that we will consider.

Cognitive neuroscience is an academic field that focuses on understanding mental processes at the neuronal level. It addresses questions of how the brain functions and what biological processes underlie thinking (cognition), feeling, and behavior.

This field developed out of important scientific contributions over the last 200 years. Most notably, early work by Paul Broca and Carl Wernicke in the nineteenth century showed that specific areas of the brain (unsurprisingly known as the Broca and Wernicke areas) are essential for specific functions. Patients who have lesions in those frontal lobe areas, for example, have difficulty either speaking or understanding what they are being told.

Then, in the early twentieth century, the work of Nobel Prize winners Santiago Ramon y Cajal and Camilo Golgi showed that the brain is formed of individual cells, called neurons. These are interconnected and pass information in the form of electrical signals from one to another, in unidirectional fashion and within nuclei or specific areas in the brain.

The actual term, *cognitive neuroscience,* was coined by George Miller and Michael Gazzaniga (more of him later in the book) in the late 1970s. Miller was the founder—together with Jerome Bruner—of the Center of Cognitive Studies at Harvard, and is now teaching at Princeton University's Department of Psychology. He is the author of one of the most frequently cited papers in psychology, *The Magical Number Seven, Plus or Minus Two* (Miller 1956). This paper suggests that seven (plus or minus two) is the magic number that characterizes people's memory performance on random lists of letters, words, numbers, or almost any kind of meaningful familiar item.

Through the use of new imaging technologies such as transcranial magnetic simulation (TMS), functional magnetic resonance imaging (fMRI), positron emission tomography (PET), and single photon emission computed tomography (SPECT), cognitive neuroscience has, over the past decade, developed an increasing body of findings that link the functioning of the brain with how we think, feel, and behave.

Let's start with a brief introduction to the human brain and a short recap of how neurons work. I believe that we can derive important insights from a better understanding of the functioning of the brain and of the interactions between neurons (the cells of the nervous system).

The Human Brain

The brain is the center of the nervous system. It monitors and regulates the body's actions and reactions, and is the center of our thinking and feeling.

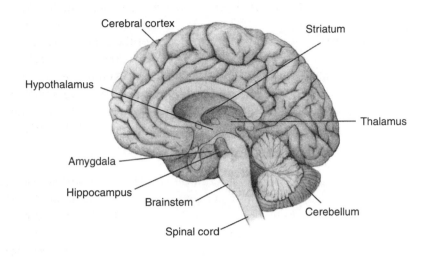

Cerebral cortex

Striatum

Hypothalamus

Thalamus

Amygdala

Hippocampus

Brainstem

Cerebellum

Spinal cord

FIGURE 5.1 The Human Brain

It is an egg-shaped object, weighing roughly 1.5 kg, with a consistency similar to soft gelatin. Although it represents only 2 percent of body weight, it consumes 20 percent of total body oxygen and 25 percent of total body energy (glucose, in fact). It has the same general structure as the brains of other vertebrates but is more than three times as large as the brain of a typical mammal with an equivalent body size, with the vast majority of the difference due to the large size of the human cerebral cortex (more on the cortex later).

If we look at the cross-section of the human brain (Figure 5.1) it becomes clear that it is composed of different areas with different forms and distribution. Broadly speaking, these different areas also have different functions, which become plain when imaging technologies are used to visualize the intensity of their activity or when they are experimentally or accidentally impaired (as discussed, for example, in the works of Broca and Wernicke).

A well-known example of accidental impairment is that of Phineas Gage, a nineteenth-century American railroad worker. During routine rock blasting, the tamping iron he used was accidentally propelled through his left cheek bone and out at the top of his head (diagonally). Phineas did not die and, in fact, could speak and walk shortly after the mishap. After two months of recovery, he was physically well. But his behavior had changed dramatically. Previously a well-balanced, shrewd person, Phineas became aggressive, impatient, and capricious. While it was not clear which areas of his brain were actually affected, "he was no longer Gage," as his doctor put it.

Let's take a closer look at the broader areas of the brain, starting from the inner parts (Pink 2006; Precht 2007; Bolte Taylor 2008; Linden 2010).

The *brainstem,* along with the spinal cord, is involved in a wide variety of sensory functions (vision, hearing, smell, taste, balance), and in managing and regulating fundamental functions of the body (for example, regulating body temperature, blood pressure, heartbeat, breathing, and digestion). It also manages important reflexes such as coughing or vomiting. A lesion of the brainstem usually leads to coma or death.

Next to the brainstem is the *cerebellum,* which is responsible for the body's balance and posture, and which supports the coordination of body movements, making them fluid and precise. A lesion of the cerebellum, for example, makes movements hesitant and clumsy (ataxia).

If we move further dorsally (upward, in Figure 5.1) and anterior (forward) we encounter the *thalamus* and the *hypothalamus.* The thalamus is involved in relaying sensory information to the higher brain areas, and from them back to the body, and to the muscles in particular. The hypothalamus is the central control station responsible for maintaining the status quo of a number of body functions (homeostasis). It controls the sleep/wake cycles, eating and drinking, and the release of hormones.

The activities of the more inner and posterior parts of the brain—the brainstem, the cerebellum, the thalamus, and the hypothalamus—are largely automatic, reflexlike, and unconscious. We do not consciously think that we should breathe. Our brain automatically takes care of it. These parts of the brain are similar to what we find in most other vertebrate animals and are believed to have developed first in the evolution of our species.

As we now move up to higher and more frontal areas, the activities of the brain become gradually more deliberate, more conscious, and more complex.

We are now looking at the *limbic system,* which includes the *amygdala,* and next to it the *hippocampus.* The amygdala is important for processing emotions of fear and aggression. It is also involved in the memorization of fear-loaded events. The hippocampus is a memory center, responsible for keeping information and facts, and a critical organ for developing long-term memories. Because we share the limbic system's structure with other animals, this part of the brain is often referred to as the reptilian brain. It is interesting to note that our limbic system does not mature during our lifetime. When it is stimulated, we react like a two-year-old, even as adults (Bolte Taylor 2008).

Moving more dorsally and to the anterior we get to the *striatum* (part of what is called the *basal ganglia*). The striatum is involved in the planning and execution of movements, and in a variety of cognitive processes involving executive function. The striatum, in particular, is believed to be involved with the memorization or storage of familiar behavior, such as habits, abilities, or skills. Rewards and punishments exert their most important effects within the striatum (Rock and Schwartz 2006; Linden 2010).

Finally we reach the *cerebral cortex,* a highly developed and complex part of the brain, large parts of which are still unknown territory for neuroscience. The most recently developed part of the cortex, in evolutionary terms, is the neocortex. The neocortex is made of millions of neurons arranged in layers and connected in intricate ways. This is the outermost part of both the right and left hemispheres.

The two hemispheres are sometimes referred to as our computing, or masculine side, and our sensing, or feminine side of the brain. The left hemisphere of the neocortex is generally associated with our higher, reflective, logical, and mathematical thinking (the Type 2 thinking of Chapter 2). The right hemisphere is generally associated with our social, moral, and spiritual sentiments. Attention, awareness, thought, and consciousness all depend on the neocortex.

Neurons and Neuroplasticity

Now that we have looked at the different parts of the brain, let's go one level deeper and look briefly at neurons (Linden 2010).

The main task of neurons is to transmit electrical signals to each other over long distances. They send these signals by means of an axon, a thin fiber that extends from the neuronal cell body and travels, usually with numerous branches, to other areas of the brain or body. Axons transmit signals to other neurons through junctions called synapses. Neurons release neurotransmitters at the synaptic connections. The two neurotransmitters that are used most frequently are glutamate, which is mostly excitatory, and gamma-aminobutyric acid (GABA), which is mostly inhibitory. Other (and popularly well-known) neurotransmitters are serotonin (the happiness hormone), histamine (well known to people suffering pollen allergy), and dopamine. Psychoactive drugs such as caffeine, nicotine, cocaine, or fluoxetine (Prozac) act on neurotransmitters or their receptors at the synaptic surface.

The scale and complexity of our neuronal system is extremely impressive. Our human brain contains roughly 100 billion neurons of different shapes and forms, each of them having on average 5,000 synapses. That makes 500 trillion synapses. If they could be laid out end to end, at the age of 20, a man has nearly 180,000 kilometers' worth, and a woman nearly 150,000 kilometers' worth of axons in their brains. Considering that the distance from the moon to the earth is roughly 380,000 kilometers, the size of our neuronal network is mind-boggling (Linden 2010).

In contrast to most types of cells in the body, neurons are formed mainly before birth, and the infant brain actually contains more neurons than the adult brain, because some neurons die when they are not used.

However, throughout life, neurons remain plastic, that is, they continuously extend new branches and form new synapses. This happens in response to external stimuli, which impinge on the brain through our senses and experiences. This neuronal plasticity happens as initially tentative synapses are retained and solidified through synaptic plasticity processes such as long-term potentiation (LTP). Simply put, long-term potentiation is an enhancement in the strength of signal transmission between two neurons. This is thought to occur as the receiving neuron (postsynaptic) progressively accumulates more neurotransmitter receptors and becomes progressively more sensitive to signals from the emitting neuron (presynaptic). This ability to modify the strength of individual synapses is thought to be fundamental to encoding memories during learning and to reinforcing them in the longer term.

In other words, the brain changes, or gets rewired, throughout life. It gets rewired as a result of where it focuses its attention, the insights it develops, and the experiences it has (Linden 2010).

It is often said that, in practice, experience results in people being wired differently. This is not just an expression but is literally the way our thoughts, memories, and habits are built into our brain. "People who practice a specialty every day literally think differently, through different sets of connections, than do people who don't practice that specialty," according to the writer David Rock and the research psychiatrist Jeffrey Schwartz (Rock and Schwartz 2006). For example, professionals in different functions—finance, operations, legal, research and development, marketing, human resources—see reality differently, think differently, feel differently, and, unsurprisingly, behave differently when confronted with the same situation.

The brain is capable of impressive internal change, or plasticity (building new synapses and rewiring), in response to the challenges it faces. In *My*

Stroke of Insight, neuroanatomist Dr. Jill Bolte Taylor, spokesperson for the Harvard Brain Tissue Resource Center, describes her own experience of rebuilding the functions of her cerebral cortex after a severe hemorrhage in 1996 seriously damaged the left side of her brain (Bolte Taylor 2008).

Plasticity, Learning, and Behavioral Change

Given that the brain is so plastic and shapeable—that is, that we can rewire our brain when we need to do so (although plasticity decreases with aging)—why is it so difficult for people to change their behavior?

The answer lies in the nature of the process of learning (building long-term memory) and two connected processes, one that inhibits learning, and one that accelerates it.

The Process of Learning

When we learn, our brain needs signals that say, "This is important. Take note!" Emotions such as joy, love, sadness, anger, and fear are such signals (Linden 2010). For example, a person may remember, sometimes after many decades, almost minute by minute, a particular day or event in which something of high (positive or negative) emotional intensity occurred (for example, winning the final at an important tennis tournament, being told that a close relative died, or even an intense public event, such as the Kennedy assassination or the terrorist attacks on September 11, 2001). But the same person may not remember anything that happened in the days before or after that event. In other words, events and experiences that are accompanied by emotionality will result in more consolidated memories.

Furthermore, when learning, our brain strengthens memories in a process of repetition, a process that neurologists call *consolidation.* Continuous repetition of a thought or a behavior leads the brain to memorize it.

Here is how it works in simple terms: We start learning new skills, habits, and behaviors through attention, a process of reflective thinking, in which new synapses, that is, new neuronal connections, are formed. We have seen that this thinking is broadly hosted in the cerebral cortex. The use of imaging technologies has shown that the reflective system activates the prefrontal cortex in particular. Activities carried out through this part of the brain require attention and concentration, and tend to consume a significant amount of energy (glucose).

Like the working memory of a personal computer, the prefrontal cortex can hold only a limited amount of information. Therefore, activities that are carried out repetitively to the extent that they become habits (consolidated as strong neuronal connections) are stored and pushed down into our "C-drive," into the automatic system. Again, imaging technologies have been used to show that an automatic system activates the hippocampus, which is involved in storing memory, as well as the striatum. The striatum is believed to steer habitual activities and procedures that are carried out without energy or effort, or, as we might say, "without much thought" (Rock and Schwartz 2006; Linden 2010).

To illustrate this, let's take a tennis player. The player wants to learn to hit the ball with a top-spin backhand (as Rafael Nadal, one of the world's best tennis players, usually hits the ball). To begin with, playing a top-spin backhand will require a great deal of attention and concentration (and produce much pleasure when hit well!). The player will need to concentrate on the footwork, on turning the trunk correctly, on the movement of the arm. In this phase, the reflective system is at work. But then, after the backhand has been played a thousand times, it becomes a routine. The footwork, the right position of the trunk, and the right swing seem to happen as if by magic, without much thinking. This is because it is now stored in the automatic system.

The Learning Inhibitor

As mentioned earlier, emotion plays a key role in learning. The amygdala is essential to this process, as it modulates emotional reactions by triggering the release of different neurotransmitters, which in turn activate other brain areas where memory is stored (for example, the hippocampus). In response to stressful situations, such as imminent danger, the amygdala can be activated very rapidly (bypassing other areas of the brain) and replace reflective thinking and learning. When we are in situations of stress or danger, instincts seem to take over (and, in fact, they do).

In contrast, when the incoming stimulus is perceived as familiar, the amygdala is calm and the adjacent hippocampus is capable of learning and memorizing new information (Rock and Schwartz 2006; Bolte Taylor 2008).

Let's go back to the tennis player. If we now try to change the backhand stroke again, we will see that the player—whenever under pressure to win the point—will automatically revert to playing the stroke as it has been played a thousand times. The player will not feel comfortable playing the new stroke when under pressure.

The same dynamics occur when people are confronted with the stress of an organizational change that requires a change of behavior. Many of the routines in an organization—how people interact, how they work, the decisions they take—are habits like those typically steered by the striatum. Changing those habits takes a lot of energy, attention, and effort. Under pressure and in situations of stress, people feel uncomfortable, resist change, and revert to more primal, or basic, behavior.

Managers sometimes underestimate the feeling of anxiety and fear that can be caused by a negative change of context, such as news about bankruptcies in an industry, a recession that costs some close friend or relative a job, or the news that the organization one works in is to be restructured. Negatively perceived change creates discomfort and diminishes the brain's ability to learn and to adapt to the new situation.

The Learning Accelerator

In contrast, a process that facilitates learning is to exploit the brain's innate desire to build new synapses or connections. More often than not, managers expect employees to change their behavior because they have been told to do so, and perhaps been given incentives. However, changing behavior is an act of learning. Brains have an innate desire to learn, to develop, and to create new neuronal connections through synapses. When people solve problems, when they learn (and create synapses) by being exposed to new ideas and stimuli, they meet the perfect conditions for the brain's innate plasticity.

If learning occurs under a strong positive emotion (that is, the pleasure of having solved a problem), it can counteract the consequences of change-induced stress or anxiety, and provide the conditions for a process of strengthening the neuronal connections, and of embedding change (and memory) in the brain.

It seems that the good old Socratic method of getting people to develop solutions by asking them questions rather than teaching them answers resonates well with the way our brain functions (Rock and Schwartz 2006).

Large-Scale Rewiring of Brains

Armed with a better understanding of the human brain and of neuroplasticity, let's now derive some implications for management. How can leaders address the mental rigidities, not just of one person, but of several thousand, or at least of those in positions critical for the change required by an organization? In other words, how can management change mental routines on a large scale?

First, management may want to provide a positive frame, or context for change. Rather than painting a doom-and-gloom picture of reality, and articulating why the firm is failing, management may need to paint a convincing, exciting, and engaging picture of the journey ahead. As we saw in Chapter 2, framing matters. To make the change story appealing, leaders need to frame it positively. This helps to reduce the stress and the anxiety level, and sets the preconditions for creativity, learning, and change (while keeping the many amygdala at bay).

Steve Jobs's turnaround at Apple shows the impact of telling a story that is simple, positive, and emotional. When he returned to the company after a long exile, he reframed the image of Apple from being a marginalized player fighting for a small percentage of market share to the home of a small, but enviable, elite: the creators who dared to "Think different" (Deutschman 2005).

Second, management may create the organizational preconditions for people to solve problems, to generate insights from within. *Self-managed teams,* such as the kaizen at Toyota, have proven to be a good vehicle for creating the conditions for continuous learning and improvement, and to be more innovative and more adaptive than other forms of organization.

Another example of people solving problems together and enhancing creativity comes from Pixar, the makers of *Toy Story, Finding Nemo,* and, more recently, *Up.* Pixar has won more than 20 Oscars. Creativity is the product that Pixar sells. It cannot afford to depend solely on its founders (Ed Catmull and John Lasseter) for it, but rather needs to deploy the creativity of the entire organization. Pixar's approach to creativity is based on two main pillars.

One, people before projects, ensures that creative individuals are brought together to generate new ideas and new projects, and to learn from one another's experience. They generate the projects rather than the projects being generated (and assigned) for them.

The other, people working together, ensures that all projects and unfinished work are shared broadly so that the network of brains providing and receiving constructive criticism is as broad as possible (100 billion neurons times the number of people at Pixar . . .).

Daniel Denison—a professor of management and organization at IMD, the International Institute for Management Development, in Lausanne, Switzerland—found that higher levels of employee participation were correlated with better organizational performance (Denison 1990). The re-cent rise of lean management techniques, in essence, the application of Toyota's kaizen approach to other industries, and to functions other than manufacturing, may be a reflection of this. We return to this later in the book.

Third, management may help peoples' insights to develop into routines, and thus into changed behavior. *Embedding insights into processes* that are repeatedly performed (changing a form or procedure so that people are obliged to continuously repeat a changed activity) is an example.

Another approach is to use learning sessions. Lean teams involve people in developing an understanding of their processes and how to continuously improve them. In workplace sessions that occur daily—typically at the start of the day—people systematically talk about ideas for making things better. They make changes to processes, and in doing so, they train their brains to make new neuronal connections.

■ ■ ■

In the case of AHD, it had become obvious to Carl that convincing the other leaders of the need for change, aligning the board and the GET on the challenges ahead, developing a new strategy, and role modeling the new strategy was all very necessary, but it wasn't sufficient.

Carl shared the insights from his dinner conversation on *rewiring* people with the six members of the GET and engaged them in a debate on how to engrain the new OPEN strategy in the heads and behaviors of AHD's key employees. It wasn't a very long debate. They concluded that they would have to engage a broader set of people in solving the problems that AHD was facing and in embedding the solutions into the day-to-day way that people worked.

In June 2006, a week or so after Carl's dinner with Andrew and his other friends, he worked with the GET to set up a new process—Carl called it the OPEN architecture process—that involved the top 50 people in the organization, deployed in 12 working groups. The working groups were organized by key accounts: the four largest customers of each AHD busi-ness unit—hospitals, dental surgeons, diagnostic centers—that represented 10 percent of AHD's total sales. The teams also included the sales represen-tatives serving these customers.

Mike, Sergei, and Mark shepherded the four teams in each of their respective areas, and Sergei took some extra time with the salespeople involved in the overall effort. John marshaled a few key people from AHD's international offices and, as needed to address customer concerns, Arthur brought in relevant managers from the manufacturing side, so each team had five to seven members.

The GET asked the 12 working groups to visit and interview their key customers, so they would understand their needs more thoroughly and could develop plans for serving them better. The GET asked the teams to make sure that their plans included proposals for optimally tailoring the product and service offerings to each customer, and making use of the open architecture framework and the full breadth of AHD's and its strategic partners' range of products and services.

Developing these proposals was an intense and, to some extent, creative process that required the teams to get involved in significant debate and problem solving. Some of the teams' discussions became very tense, especially when—after reviewing customer needs—they deemed a product or service sourced from a strategic partner to be superior to an in-house solution. The process was, however, also very engaging and fruitful. Some of the proposals were very innovative and produced immediate sales increases when presented to the customers.

The exercise was clearly a success, not only for the quality of the new ideas and innovative solutions it generated, but because when it was done, the open architecture philosophy was ingrained into the brains of AHD's top people. Reactions from the 12 major customers involved were overwhelmingly positive; their leaders felt that AHD now really understood their needs, and most of them increased their orders.

The GET members and the other managers involved in the project understood that they had to go further to make the change stick. They institutionalized the 12-team process and made it continuous. Every month, the teams would provide feedback on how their customer relationships were developing and discuss proposals for developing them even further.

As a result of the team reports, AHD created a tool box, a set of forms that would help consistently and coherently articulate the way the company would investigate and analyze customer needs, develop and package its OPEN offerings, and approach customers. By December 2006, six months later, the new process and the OPEN toolbox had become a way of life at AHD, a de facto *standard operating procedure* for working with key customers.

As sales to these 12 crucial customers soared, Carl grew increasingly confident in his ability to transform the fortunes of AHD. He had reformed the board and the GET, and developed the new OPEN strategy that involved a high level of collaboration with partners to market best-of-breed offerings to AHD's customers, and would accelerate the geographic expansion of

AHD. After some initial setbacks, the strategy seemed to work, and when piloted with 12 large accounts, it had produced significant sales increases.

The year-end results for 2006 showed an improvement on the year before, and the sales data for the fourth quarter of 2006 showed that AHD had started to regain market share in all three product lines.

"AHD is starting to rock," said Carl to Gwen one evening, reflecting on the achievements in his first two years as AHD's CEO. "I am doing a great job. I am turning the situation around. I am really proud of how AHD is changing. I . . ."

However, things were about to change, big time.

In early 2007, Carl was diagnosed with cancer.

In just over a week, with Gwen by his side, he learned that his cancer was developing slowly but was incurable. He would receive chemotherapy, with the objective of prolonging his life. The prognosis was that he had another 5 to 10 years to live, a period during which he would enjoy good mental and physical condition.

It was a huge shock. He felt as if he'd been hit by a truck. Suddenly everything changed, prompting a myriad of questions that he had never before asked himself.

Why? Why was it happening to him? Was it genetic? Was it due to stress? His doctors had no answer. It probably didn't matter, anyway. It was what it was. He had to live with it.

His thoughts then focused on his family, on Gwen and the children. It was tough for them, no doubt. But would they be at least well-off? Could they stand on their own feet? He checked all his insurance policies and took stock of the family's assets. And yes, he thought that at least financially the family was fine.

So, what should he do with his remaining years?

He had worked hard all his life to become a CEO. He was competitive and ambitious, and he wanted to prove he could be a great CEO, a great leader. AHD was struggling, so he hadn't yet proven he could be a successful CEO of a company that size. But what was the point of proving it now?

Should he use his remaining years to do something else? What else?

He and Gwen had always dreamt of a home in Tuscany overlooking a vineyard. The previous summer, during their vacation in Italy, they had spent some time looking for houses. At the time, buying a house in Italy did not fit their plans. But now? Shouldn't they spend their time together, with their children in the place they liked best and get the most out of it?

He was haunted by a thought from Socrates, the Greek philosopher, who said that the unexamined life is not worth living. How could Carl make sure he wasn't just wasting the years he still had to live? How could he live a life that mattered?

He spent weeks talking to colleagues and friends. He spent time in a library reading everything that seemed relevant to him, from biology, psychology, and neurology, to philosophy, looking for answers to his questions.

He also turned to religion. He spent several days in the Holy Trinity Monastery in Alabama, debating with William, the abbot, who was a close friend. Having been in the same college, Carl and William shared many memories. Although they had later followed different paths, they continued to remain friends and to meet occasionally. Religion ultimately provides meaning to life, and many of Carl's friends who were religious seemed to live fulfilled lives. But Carl wasn't religious.

He couldn't find the answers he was looking for.

While he was still searching for answers to the problem he now faced, Carl was surprised to receive a call from Deni, a former colleague at KenkoInc. He was a junior member of the management team, one of the first people whom Carl had recruited when he had moved to Osaka to help set up KenkoInc many years ago. After saying hello, Deni explained, "I actually called to say 'thank you,' Carl." Carl didn't understand: "Why, Deni? What are you thanking me for?"

Deni explained, "We've just gone through the mill with a quality problem with one of our key products. As it turned out, the problem had repercussions and the issue grew bigger and bigger within a matter of days." Deni described being under siege by lawyers, and told Carl, "This whole problem was starting to seriously hurt the company. Things looked really bad. We were worried. But then one of the people on the management team asked: 'What would Carl do if he were here?'"

"That changed the whole game," Deni said. "We decided to do what we thought you would have done."

KenkoInc's managers then analyzed and acknowledged the seriousness of their problem, went public with it, and reimbursed all the customers who had suffered losses. The exemplary way they handled the crisis strengthened KenkoInc's reputation for customer service even further. It was a big success.

"That's why I am calling to say thank you," Deni concluded. "What you taught us over many years guided us. We mastered this difficult situation. We knew that we could do it. And we did it. This is your legacy, Carl. Thank you so much."

This moment was an eye-opener. Carl realized that he had just heard something profound, and that a whole new world was about to unfold.

Carl's time in Osaka had been very fulfilling. He had hired almost all of KenkoInc's sales and marketing employees personally, at least during his first years there. He had made all of the important decisions: which markets to enter, which customers to serve, what product portfolio to develop and market.

He remembered that while in Japan, he often spoke about KenkoInc as if it were his baby, his third child. Carl had helped develop KenkoInc into a firm that had the right purpose, the right people, and the right values. He had built a cadre of people who were able to master difficulties they confronted effectively and with self-confidence.

Carl's next years would not be about himself. They wouldn't be about proving anything to anyone. They wouldn't be about personal triumph.

They would be about his legacy. About giving, teaching, helping. They would be about building the self-confidence and the ability of others, of his family and of people he cared for.

He also realized that as the head of a company he had one great opportunity: to lead the same transformation for many people, or even for an entire firm. "At scale," he thought. The idea was profound and energizing.

He decided that he wanted to continue to lead AHD. He wouldn't hide the diagnosis or the fact that he was receiving chemotherapy. He informed the board and the members of the GET, sitting down with them one by one. Hubert, the senior director, encouraged him to continue to lead AHD if he had the energy to do so.

Carl had the energy, and he wanted to carry on. He wanted to transform AHD into an organization that would be as strong, as capable, and as self-confident as KenkoInc. It meant building a successful firm, a firm with a purpose, a firm with values, a firm with proud people who had the capabilities and the self-confidence to succeed. He wanted to reproduce KenkoInc at scale—a substantial challenge, given that AHD was about 10 times larger than the company he had helped build in Osaka.

Scale meant that—as a first step—he now needed to go beyond the top 50 individual executives and beyond the 12 biggest customers. He wanted to extend the new approach—the OPEN strategy—to the entire organization, to reach all of its customers and all of its employees.

The new modus operandi for implementing the OPEN concept required a much higher level of cross-unit collaboration across the entire firm. This was a problem for AHD. John's country organizations; the three product business units under Sergei, Mark, and Mike (including their individual research and product development arms); Arthur's manufacturing plants; Monica's finance and human resource departments; and the information technology support function hardly collaborated at all. John, Arthur, and, particularly, Monica had to have somewhat of an overview, given the nature of their jobs, but generally AHD's departments were all in their own separate silos, linking up at lower management levels and only when necessary. Collaboration between them (and with external parties) was notoriously poor.

In the spring of 2007, Carl decided to introduce three new global customer-focused units—hospitals, clinics, and dental surgeons—to integrate and develop customer solutions across the three product groups (orthopedics, dental, and diagnostics), research and development, and manufacturing. The idea was that these three global customer-segment functions would be responsible for developing the best possible client offerings by applying the open architecture concept. Carl soon realized that these customer segment units needed to be closer to the market, and he replicated them within John's country organizations.

The new units necessitated a new set of processes. The three units would now develop customer segment strategies and plans. This would mean adjusting AHD's annual strategic and operational review process, and would provide input into its research and product development efforts.

Adding the three customer segment units was a very innovative move and had enormous benefits. The new organization produced better insights about customer behavior; information Sergei's, Mike's, and Mark's departments could apply in a targeted way to improve service quality. The new units fed their improved insights into research and worked with Arthur's manufacturing experts to develop new technologies and products that would better satisfy customer demands. Now, AHD could create better product bundles. Finally, it could target sales efforts more precisely, on the basis of customer needs and potential customer profitability.

It was a great idea, and when Carl presented it at the annual Investors Day seminar, the analysts applauded.

Soon, however, Carl started noticing something less satisfactory. Somehow, the organization had become very sluggish. People were spending hours traveling to internal sales conferences, manufacturing alignment meetings, finance best-practice round-tables, and the like. AHD employees were constantly in internal meetings, on the phone to each other, or sending e-mails from one department to another. There was a sense that hardly anything was actually getting done beyond this internal churn.

And a strange story was making the rounds of the corridors. It probably wasn't true. But maybe it was. It was the story of a sales representative who—stuck in internal alignment meetings, coordination task forces, initiative groups, and so on—hadn't seen a customer for a whole year. Some found the story amusing, but not Carl. What was going on?

The culprit was quickly found: too much bureaucracy. The burden of bureaucracy had already been an issue before the introduction of the three customer segment units, but it seemed to have grown exponentially since. It was now on everybody's mind. In town hall meetings or individual discussions, employees repeatedly confronted Carl with their concerns about bureaucracy.

Capturing the sentiment in the organization, the head of the human resources department sent a report to the members of the GET. Its title was "Blow Up Bureaucracy!"

The report had been produced by the human resources department with the help of an external research firm called Beyond Structure Associates (BSA), which focused on themes of human resources and organization.

BSA had studied the situation carefully and recommended discarding the current organizational structure and replacing it with what they called a *learning organization* of loosely connected independent, self-directed individuals. The new organization would thrive on virtual collaboration platforms. It would foster improvisation, learning, and creativity.

Somewhere in the report Carl read, "The new organization will foster freedom at the expense of structure. It will focus on the outside at the expense of the inside."

"Oh my God," Carl thought. "This is at least as much BS as the presentation on peak performance of a few years ago." And again, by BS he didn't mean Beyond Structure.

Carl felt as if every time he solved one big problem, another one cropped up to take its place.

A few weeks later, one day in early summer 2007, Carl received a note from an employee, Dr. Alicia Dubitsky. He did not know Dr. Dubitsky, so he admired her initiative and courage in writing a personal note to him. She was a network manager in the information technology department. She had joined AHD only a few months ago, with a PhD in network theory from Columbia University. Her note contained an insightful analysis of the current organizational structure and a number of recommendations for simplifying the organization and improving the situation. It was very thought-provoking.

PART III

Organizational Rigidities

CHAPTER 6

Long Live Bureaucracy!

When Arnold Schwarzenegger took office in 2003 as the new governor of the State of California, the state budget was running a huge deficit. In his state of the state address on June 1, 2004, he identified one of the causes to be the ineffective, slow, and inefficient government system: "The Executive Branch of this government is a mastodon frozen in time and about as responsive. This is not the fault of our public servants but of the system. We have multiple departments with overlapping responsibilities. I say consolidate them. We have boards and commissions that serve no pressing public need. I say abolish them. We have a state purchasing program that is archaic and expensive. I say modernize it." With a strong Austrian accent, he put forward the essence of his approach as follows: "Every governor proposes moving boxes around to reorganize government. I don't want to move boxes around; I want to blow them up" (Schwarzenegger 2004).

In the previous three chapters we have reviewed three factors that reduce the ability of individuals to adapt to changing situations: mental biases, lack of (task-specific) self-confidence, and inflexible brain connections. And we have shown how these individual rigidities can adversely affect the ability of organizations to address the challenges they are facing.

Let's now focus our attention on groups of individuals, on organizations. In this chapter, we look at the first of five organizational rigidities: dense organizational structures, or—to use a more popular term—bureaucracy.

In discussions, managers often blame the lack of organizational adaptation and change on bureaucracy.

Dense structures may prevent senior managers from receiving vital information from the front line of the organization. Front-line salespeople may lose business to competitors, which the firm might be able to recapture with a small change to the product. But the information is filtered several times and may never reach the CEO. Also, many CEOs feel that their decisions are slowed down, and sometimes even stalled, by dense structures. Information that would provide guidance gets lost in the organization, much to the CEO's frustration.

Academics share these perspectives. Dense hierarchies lead to ossification and organizational death (Hannan and Freeman 1977, 1989; Leonard-Barton 1992; Loderer, Neusser, and Waelchli 2009). The advice: Let's simplify and unlayer, let's flatten the organization and increase spans of control. In short, bureaucracy is passé, let's blow it up.

This is a very simplistic perspective, and a dangerous one. While it is clear that dense organizational structures slow down adaptation and change, we need to develop a more nuanced and articulated perspective on hierarchies before we touch them, let alone blow them up. We need to understand why, in the first place, organizations exist, and why they need bureaucracy to function.

Why Organizations Exist

In *The Nature of the Firm,* a highly influential article published in 1937, Ronald Coase, a British economist and now Clifton R. Musser Professor Emeritus of Economics at the University of Chicago Law School, developed a theory to explain why the economy is made up of a number of firms instead of consisting of independent and self-employed individuals. Given that in a free and efficient market "production could be carried on without any organization that is, firms at all," Coase noticed, why do firms emerge? (Coase 1937).

The traditional economic theory of the time suggested that in an efficient market, where those who are best at performing an activity specialize in it and offer their services to others, it would be less expensive to contract products or activities out than to hire people and build organizations.

Coase pointed out, however, that there are a series of transaction costs when buying services and activities in the market. When a service or an activity is sourced from the market, significant costs are incurred above and beyond the cost of the service or activity. There are search costs involved, negotiation costs, legal costs of setting up a contract, monitoring costs (are the contractual obligations being fulfilled?), and enforcement costs. Coase suggested that firms emerge when organizations try to avoid these transaction costs. They produce services and products in-house.

There is, however, a natural limit to what can be provided or produced in-house. Coase noticed that increasing overhead costs, increasing complexity, and an increasing probability that an overloaded CEO will err in allocating resources effectively and efficiently set a natural limit to how large a firm can become. He called this "decreasing returns to the entrepreneur function."

Coase argued that the optimum size of a firm is reached when the sum of the transaction costs (which decrease with the size of a firm) and of the complexity costs (which increase with the size of the firm) is lowest.

Coase received the Nobel Prize for Economics in 1991.

Chaos or Bureaucracy

Now that we understand why firms exist, why do they need bureaucracy— that is, organizational structures?

Let's start with an illustration.

Let's assume that a firm has 20 senior managers. Let's also assume that the organization wants to align all of its senior members on one decision. In the extreme case, without any hierarchy, everyone would have to meet everyone else, and that would require [n * (n − 1)]/2, meetings, that is, 190 meetings. This would take forever.

But in a hierarchical organization things happen much more quickly and easily. Assume that the firm is organized into three layers: one CEO, three divisional heads, and five or six departments per division. It would take just four meetings to get everyone aligned: three divisional meetings, and one meeting of the divisional heads with the CEO (Figure 6.1).

Things become even worse if more people are involved in the decision-making process. Let's assume that the organization has 100 senior managers. With no hierarchy it would need 4,950 meetings to align everyone on a given decision! This might take several months. In contrast, if we assume four layers only (and a team size at the bottom of five to six employees) it would need only 19 meetings to get everyone aligned.

The alternative to hierarchy is chaos. In network theory, hierarchy reduces the density of connections and allows networks to grow in size and to function effectively, which is also why even with computers (where meetings happen in fractions of seconds) networks are organized hierarchically (Beinhocker 2006).

Organizational structures are how firms organize their work. Hierarchies allow firms to organize the work of thousands of people, while

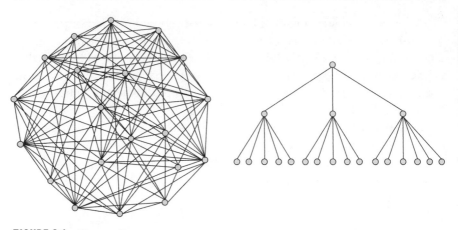

FIGURE 6.1   Chaos or Bureaucracy

Source: Adapted from Beinhocker, E. D. *The Origin of Wealth: Evolution, Complexity, and the Radical Remaking of Economics.* Boston: Harvard Business School Press, 2006.

maintaining coherence and implementing a strategy effectively. Organizational structures may be rigid and hard to change, but they allow firms to get complex tasks—tasks for which the work of a few individuals does not suffice—done. Organizational structures thus enable firms to grow to very considerable size.

A Matter of Interdependencies

Now that we have saved the hierarchy from being blown up, let's study it more closely. Why is it that some firms develop more dense hierarchies and some less? Why do some firms work with four organizational layers and others need eight to perform, even though they may have a similar number of employees?

Scott Page, the director of the Center for the Study of Complex Systems at the University of Michigan, believes that the depth of organizational structures depends on the complexity of the strategy that a firm is trying to implement.

He believes that if the strategy can be easily broken down into parallel tasks, and not much coordination between the tasks is needed, then the organization will be relatively flat. An advertising agency typically has a very flat structure. Its projects are usually for different customers, they can be carried out in parallel, and require very little coordination (maybe some common firm policies), and hence almost no hierarchy.

On the other hand, if the strategy cannot be easily broken up into parallel tasks, and there are many interdependencies between tasks, requiring significant coordination, then organizations will tend to be narrow and deep. Car manufacturers typically have very dense organizational structures. The activities of the various units—from market research, product design, manufacturing of components, sourcing of components, marketing, dealer management, sales, and so on—can be done only partly in parallel. Also, the activities of the various units are highly interdependent and significant coordination is required (what if the different pieces don't fit together when the car is finally assembled?).

Page's explanation helps us understand why firms in different industries tend to have different organizational charts and models (Page 1996; Beinhocker 2006).

Large and Complex Modern Organizations

Individuals involved in software design know the issue of growth and density of interactions: a software program, once designed with a simple structure, grows and becomes more complex as time goes by, as the programmer adds overlays and additional algorithms for the program to solve additional tasks and requirements posed by the user. As a consequence of increased density of interactions, however, the program becomes slow and inefficient, much to the frustration of the user.

The analogy helps us understand the malaise of many of today's large organizational models.

As a result of industry consolidation, international expansion, and diversification over the past few decades, firms have become considerably larger, more global, and more complex. In Chapter 2, we looked at the top 50 U.S. firms. In 1960, their combined revenues amounted to $103 billion, or nearly $2.1 billion per company. Fifty years later, in 2010, the combined revenues of the top 50 U.S. firms amounted to $5.1 trillion, or $102 billion per company.

To manage their business in different countries in various geographic regions, several large firms have introduced regional and subregional structures. Also, wishing to ensure the implementation of global policies and to capture economies of scale globally, many firms have strengthened their functional secondary axes, such as information technology, procurement, human resources, and finance. Many have also introduced central marketing, customer-segment, or sales channel functions to foster the exchange of best practices between countries and regions.

Organizational models originally based on simple vertical structures—a relic of Taylorism and of the industrial age—have become more complex as matrix overlays have been added to accommodate secondary management axes (sometimes several). These overlays also serve as ad hoc constructs such as study groups and innovation committees. Cross-unit product boards have also been added to the model (Bryan and Joyce 2005).

Many large firms have developed very dense and deep organizational structures with extensive interdependencies. The organizational chart of some global organizations looks like a network, and as a result, people spend endless time in meetings, on the phone, and emailing each other to align and to coordinate. The amount of time spent on internal coordination is enormous.

Similar to the software user, many leaders and employees of today's large organizations are frustrated. Their organizations have become inwardly orientated, lack innovation, and are slow in adapting to changes in the market.

Building Tomorrow's Global Organization

In recent years, the matter of organizational simplification has received much attention (Ashkenas 2007; Heywood, Spungin, and Turnbull 2007; Bryan and Joyce 2005).

Organizational design matters a lot. If an organization is designed as a complex, multilayered matrix with several units depending on one another, it will develop a deep, dense hierarchy and will be very slow to react to changes in the environment. If the same organization can be designed to implement the same strategies equally effectively with a simpler business unit or functional organization, it will be faster and more adaptive.

Three key principles govern the creation of an effective and adaptive organization.

First, *objectives and scope of organization need to be prioritized* thoughtfully. John Maeda, a graphic designer and visual artist, and the E. Rudge and Nancy Allen Professor of Media Arts and Sciences at the Massachusetts Institute of Technology Media Lab, believes that the simplest way to achieve simplicity is through the thoughtful reduction of functionalities (Maeda 2006).

He is obviously not referring to firms, but to consumer electronics devices, but we can apply his rule of simplicity to business in three ways: prioritizing organizational objectives, clarifying scope, and using skunk works.

1. *Prioritizing organizational objectives.* Firms sometimes want to achieve too many objectives with an organizational structure. For large, diversified global firms, achieving accountability, ensuring entrepreneurial freedom, enabling growth, capturing economies of scale and skills, and transferring best practices all at once is hard. A thoughtful prioritization of the organization's objectives is needed and should answer questions such as "What will be the main value drivers in the next five years?" "What do we want to change in terms of business focus in the next five years?" A thoughtful prioritization includes first and foremost the decision on the dominant axes of management—functional, product, customer, or geography. It also includes the prioritization of objectives at a secondary level. For example, once, in search of opportunities to capture economies of scale, I discussed with the CEO of a large, diversified firm the creation of shared regional services centers for specific corporate functions such as finance and human resources. "I understand the savings opportunities, but for the next few years clear accountability for results will produce more bottom-line results, and is therefore more important to me. I do not want to jeopardize that. The shared regional function will have to wait," was the CEO's answer. An example of the thoughtful reduction of objectives in practice.

2. *Clarifying scope.* Many organizations create organizational complexities by scope creep, or proliferation: launching new lines of business, constantly tweaking package designs, expanding the product range, and increasing the number of items in stock are just some examples. Making choices and setting priorities in terms of scope (for example, business portfolio strategy, product portfolio strategy, stock strategy) should be an early consideration in any organizational redesign (Ashkenas 2007).

3. *Using skunk works.* Organizations can keep parts of the business separate using so-called skunk works (a close cousin of clarifying scope). A reorganization is not always feasible; firms sometimes need to react fast and do not have the time to redesign the way people work and interact in the firm. The solution then is to use skunk works to create completely autonomous units and to separate them from the rest of the organization. This gives them the autonomy to react quickly and seize opportunities as they arise. Nespresso, for example, was initially

developed outside of Nestlé. Apple's Macintosh computer was developed by "a small autonomous team with a pirate flag flying from the mast of a separate building" (Beinhocker 2006).

Second, the number of interdependencies needs to be reduced by *creating self-managed performance cells complemented by knowledge networks*. Let's look at these two separately: first, self-managed performance cells.

Self-managed performance cells are smaller autonomous units, or notional companies. One of the first applications of this concept was the reorganization of General Motors (GM) by Alfred Sloan, its long-standing president and chairman. In the 1950s, he reorganized GM into five divisions, effectively five independent car companies, each with its own brand and its own profit and loss statement. This allowed GM to grow and—at the time—to become the world's largest corporation (Beinhocker 2006).

This concept has since been applied in many companies and industries, as they have reorganized into some form of business unit structure. In the past decade—and inspired by firms such as IBM and Procter & Gamble—several companies have started to apply the concept of the notional company to other areas as well, creating global manufacturing companies and global business support function (GBS) companies, specialized firms providing shared back-office services such as accounting, payroll services, and infrastructure services. These notional manufacturing and service companies interact with business units as they would with third parties, selling services on a contractual basis (remember Coase's theory).

Nor does the concept stop at the level of business units, or notional manufacturing and service companies. It can be applied much lower down the organizational hierarchy. Inspired by the kaizen concept at Toyota, many firms are creating more autonomous, self-managed teams in a large variety of functions. We nowadays often find them in functions such as sales, manufacturing, or back-office operations. These teams are often referred to as *lean teams*.

An extreme but illustrative example of this is Whole Foods, an American firm founded in 1980 in Austin, Texas, which is now the world's leader in natural and organic foods, with more than 270 grocery stores in North America and the United Kingdom. The entire firm is organized as a set of self-managed teams. The teams are empowered to hire, fire, and allocate bonuses within their membership. Everyone is a key decision maker, so everyone has access to all key business data. Information is shared so widely that the SEC considers all 36,000 employees as insiders for stock trading purposes!

Whatever the level at which performance cells are being set up, they share three characteristics: They are guided by performance metrics, they have the autonomy to organize themselves, and they have periodical learning cycles.

1. *Performance metrics.* Depending on the specific objectives and activities of the cells, these metrics may vary. For a business unit, there would be a scorecard, including a profit and loss statement. For lean sales or customer management teams, the metrics might include cross-selling rates, revenues, or service quality. In lean manufacturing teams, they might include default rates, scrap rates, or unit costs. When the performance metrics measure outcomes that relate directly to the desired behavior (not, for example, like the stock price, which depends on multiple factors unrelated to personal or team performance), they can form the basis for the monetary reward system for the cells and their members.

2. *Autonomy to organize themselves.* Performance cells have the ability to continuously improve the outcome or results. This means that they are delegated the responsibility for decisions on those resources that are most pertinent for achieving the objectives. A division, for example, may be allowed to organize its regional structure differently from another division. There is a significant amount of literature suggesting that autonomy or participative management should be limited and focused on the organization of the work of the cells (self-management), as opposed to cells setting their own targets and organizing their work (which we would call self-directed teams). Several studies suggest that cells that self-set their targets record higher levels of employee satisfaction, but not of performance, at least at the level of teams (Bandura 1997).

3. *Learning cycles.* Third, performance cells have periodic reflection cycles, periods of learning when new challenges are discussed, when ruthless transparency and debate is promoted (a dense information environment being used to address the mental biases of overoptimism and loss aversion), when elephants in the room are named, and when problems are jointly solved. Here, too, the solutions vary depending on the level at which performance cells are formed. In the case of a company or a large business unit, the reflection and learning cycle may be longer and take place in the context of quarterly or monthly performance review meetings. For smaller units such as lean teams, learning cycles may be shorter and occur on a daily basis. Though the term *performance review* may suggest otherwise, the sessions are better

used to reflect and learn collectively. Regardless of whether the targets are quarterly, monthly, weekly, or daily, and are met or not met, the questions should be: "What happened in the past months that we did not expect? Has our environment changed, and why? Why did we not succeed as planned? What can we learn from this? What should we do differently next time? What new challenges may we face?" They should not be: "What did you do wrong? Why did you not make the target?"

At Toyota, anyone on the production line can suggest improvements to the production process. Courageous conversations require far less courage there because critical ideas have become normalized, whereas that is far less the case on production lines in other companies (Heifetz, Grashow, and Linsky 2009).

Self-managed performance cells can be complemented by *formal knowledge networks,* which are better than hierarchy and structure at ensuring knowledge creation, management, and dissemination. People with common interests—such as similar work (supply chain managers, for example) or the same clientele (such as private-client advisers)—naturally form social networks.

Companies can capture the value of networks by investing in them and formalizing them, for example, by defining network owners and making them responsible for building knowledge and capabilities, or by providing a shared infrastructure for knowledge codification and sharing.

By capturing new insights from the different independent, self-managed units and teams, and by accessing external sources of innovation, networks generate knowledge, which is then made accessible to the organization. Industry practices in investment banks, or industry or functional practices in consulting firms exemplify such networks (Bryan and Joyce 2005, 2007).

Third, *the organization needs to build on standards.* In network theory, large networks can be created only by building on a standard, such as the HTML standard in the Internet or the GSM standard in mobile telephony. Standardization decreases the level of ambiguity, increases predictability, and allows networks to function more effectively.

In our context, standardization means using replicable models for self-managed performance cells (such as a standard country organization), standardized job descriptions, standardized job profiles, standardized approaches for key processes (the way customer research is done at Procter & Gamble is highly standardized, for example), and so forth.

Corporate functions such as finance, human resources, information technology, or sourcing play an important role in developing and enforcing standards, such as corporate policies, standardized functional job profiles and career paths, standardized functional processes such as the performance management process (for example, target setting, budgeting, controlling, and so on), and the talent development processes (for example, recruitment, appraisal and rewards, development and training, and so on).

■ ■ ■

Alicia Dubitsky's note, which Carl shared with the GET, made the point that while adding customer-segment units to the organization was a great idea in principle—it hadn't worked. It seemed to have made an ineffective organization even worse.

Her note spelled out, with precise analysis, why AHD was so complex. It started with a series of questions. Why did AHD have so much hierarchy even before the introduction of the three customer service units? The note studied the organizational changes at AHD over the past three decades.

In the early 1980s, AHD had a fairly simple organization (Figure 6.2).

AHD had developed the orthopedics business by exploiting what was then an innovative material-coating technology. It was manufacturing and selling in the United States, and through two subsidiaries, one in Germany

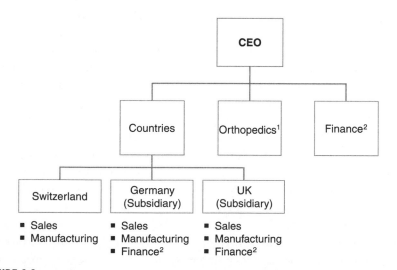

FIGURE 6.2 **Starting Point—SMP as a Rather Flat and Simple Sales-Oriented Organization**

[1]R&D, Product Development
[2]Finance, HR, Legal

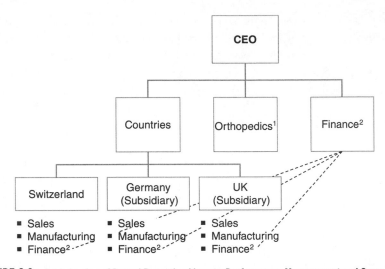

FIGURE 6.3 Introduction of Dotted Reporting Lines or Performance Management and Compliance
[1]R&D, Product Development
[2]Finance, HR, Legal

and one in the United Kingdom. It was also distributing in other countries through local distributors.

Following a bribery scandal in a German hospital in the mid-1980s and an accounting fraud in the United Kingdom, AHD decided to increase the power of its finance support function, which included accounting, human resources, and legal and compliance. To ensure compliance with internal policies and external regulations, the finance function added dotted lines to the U.S. sales organization—which was by now a separate subsidiary—and to the German and British subsidiaries (Figure 6.3).

In the second half of the 1980s, AHD had started to expand very rapidly internationally. In 1986, it founded six new subsidiaries in the United States. In 1987, it went into France, with a subsidiary in Marseille. In 1989, AHD went east, buying a small competitor in Seoul, South Korea, and setting up a subsidiary in Tokyo, Japan. By the early 1990s, AHD was in 30 countries. The organizational structure was unable to handle all these countries, so three regions—Europe, the Americas, and Asia—were set up to oversee the activities of the 30 subsidiaries. The regions would be responsible for managing the countries' performance (target setting, monitoring, and appraisal), while the finance central support function (accounting, human resources, legal and compliance) would continue to ensure compliance with internal policies and external regulations in all countries (Figure 6.4).

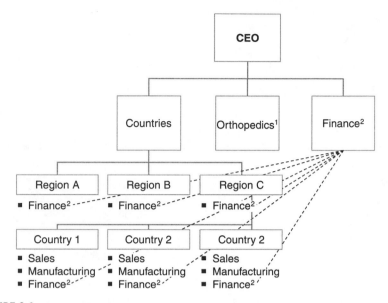

FIGURE 6.4   Geographical Expansion and Introduction of Regions
[1]R&D, Product Development
[2]Finance, HR, Legal

In 1992, AHD entered the point of care (POC) diagnostics business through the acquisition of DiagnostiCo in the United States. The idea was to exploit AHD's commercial capabilities and access to clinics and hospitals to develop the POC diagnostics business, which promised to grow rapidly in the years ahead. Until the mid-1990s, DiagnostiCo was essentially a U.S. business, but by the end of the decade, AHD had taken it global, boosting it on the back of its presence in, now, 50 countries.

In some countries, the orthopedics and the diagnostics business units shared the country sales organization. In others—especially in larger countries—they each had a dedicated country sales organization reporting to them, as shown on the organizational chart with a dotted line.

In the mid-1990s, AHD set up MedCo, a dental implant business, again exploiting its commercial capabilities. The commercial synergies did not prove to be as strong as expected, and AHD found it had to maintain and expand a dedicated sales organization for the dental business, addressing primarily dental surgeons (Figure 6.5). Despite this apparent setback, AHD was now in the dental business, which started to grow very rapidly in the second part of the 1990s.

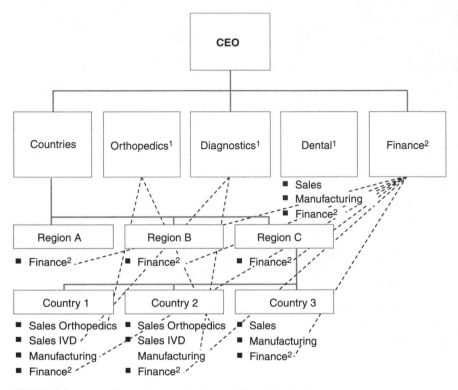

FIGURE 6.5 Acquisition and Integration of an Additional Product Line
[1]R&D, Product Development
[2]Finance, HR, Legal

AHD hired Arthur in 2000 as the new head of manufacturing for the U.S. operation, which now included four plants. He came from outside the industry; he had been the head of manufacturing at CarCo in Europe. He brought many new ideas. One of them was to make better use of AHD's manufacturing network (by now it had 30 plants in 18 countries), specializing plants by technology and capturing economies of scale. He promised cost savings of 10 percent and better product quality. It was a no-brainer. His position was strengthened, and dotted lines going from Arthur's unit to all plants were added to the organizational structure (Figure 6.6).

And then came Carl. With his customer-centric open architecture approach, and with the OPEN strategy, he added three customer segment units—dental surgeons, clinics, and hospitals—to the organization at the global and regional level.

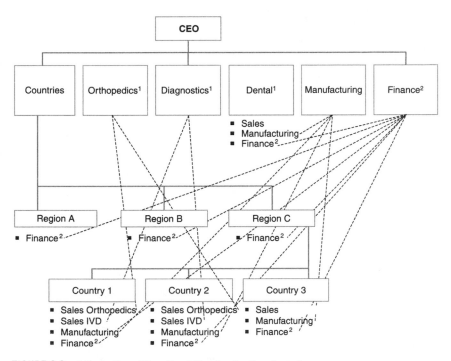

FIGURE 6.6　**Introduction of Functional Steering for Manufacturing**
[1]R&D, Product Development
[2]Finance, HR, Legal

Dr. Dubitsky's note had included one chart, showing all the dotted lines (Figure 6.7). It was a mess! No wonder everyone was complaining and nothing was getting done. The organizational structure looked like the marriage of a spider's web and a large network. The hierarchy was enormously dense.

When the members of the GET listened to Carl and studied Dr. Dubitsky's spider web chart, they realized why it was hard to understand who was responsible for what. Accountabilities were completely blurred. Whenever a client complained about a faulty product or service, a merry-go-round finger-pointing ceremony would take place. "It was the product line's fault," Sales would say. "No, it was Manufacturing's fault," the product line would answer. "Manufacturing? No way! The specs were wrong," Manufacturing would say. "Specs? Absolutely not. It was an explicit request from Sales," the product line would counter.

It was very frustrating. The GET members felt that whenever there was a success—a new product launched successfully; a new, large account

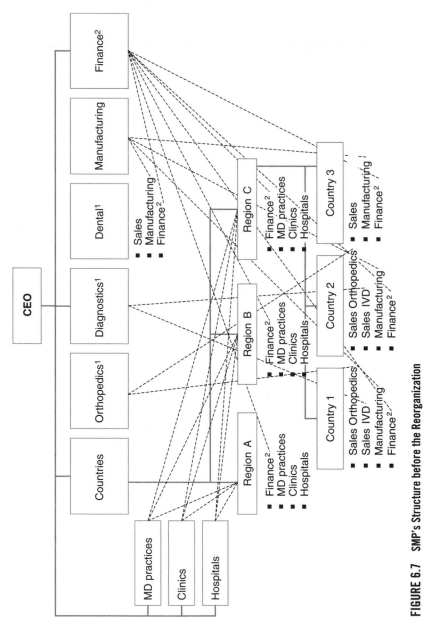

FIGURE 6.7 SMP's Structure before the Reorganization

[1]R&D, Product Development
[2]Finance, HR, Legal

won—plenty of people were ready to claim responsibility. But not when things went wrong. "Success has many parents; failure is an orphan," Carl thought.

It was time to redesign the organizational structure. But how? Dr. Dubitsky's note provided some ideas. The GET team expanded on it by studying organizational models and ideas recently introduced by comparable global firms. They went looking for inspiration and new ideas. They then put what they found into practice.

Specifically, they made the following changes:

- Dental was already by and large a separate unit within AHD. The dental business unit had its own sales organization in every country. Its reps visited primarily dental surgeons, while clinics and hospitals were essentially the domain of the other two product lines, orthopedics and diagnostics. Other synergies were also limited, and other than the initial inability to exploit commercial capabilities across the various product segments, AHD had not made much effort to get the dental business to collaborate with the other two product lines. Inspired by the story of General Motors, and by Alfred Sloan, who created five separate companies at GM, with separate brands, AHD's top team decided to separate the dental unit into an autonomous company. They transferred the various national dental sales functions, the dental manufacturing plants, and the central dental product unit into a separate company, Dental Inc. Sergei, who continued to be a member of the GET, was appointed as CEO of Dental Inc. He was very happy.

- Inspired by the Global Business Support division of Procter & Gamble, the GET decided to transfer all back-office services provided by the support functions of Monica's finance, human resources, and legal departments to a separate division. This separate division—called AHD Global Business Support Functions, or simply, GBS—would provide unified, standardized services such as payment services, accounting, personnel administration, and legal-file management to both Dental Inc. and AHD. GBS would also manage the offshoring center that AHD had built close to Mumbai in the late 1990s. It had never been well managed or well used, and had long been plagued with high turnover rates. As interfaces became simpler, with GBS as its sole customer, and with a better design for its outsourced activities, the offshoring center also started to do well. As Monica had predicted, overall savings in the back-office support areas amounted to nearly 30 percent by the third year after the changes. She was relieved to have the back-office functions segmented and welcomed the appointment of Vijai, a U.S.-trained Indian outsourcing expert, as CEO of GBS and a new member of the GET. (Vijai, a knowledgeable cricket fan who was fluent in six languages, became the youngest member of the GET, a distinction Carl was glad to relinquish.)

- The economies of scale in manufacturing were too big to ignore. Following the example of IBM, AHD set up a separate contract manufacturing company, called AHD Manufacturing, or simply AHDM. AHDM would produce equipment for AHD's two business units, dental implants and orthopedics. As a consequence, the unit costs for implants fell 21 percent by the third year after the changes. Arthur was appointed CEO of AHDM, while remaining a member of the GET.

- Finally, the GET split AHD's sales channels into two streams and merged sales with the product lines in orthopedics and diagnostics, effectively creating two notional companies within AHD. They called the two units *divisions*. They had separate sales organizations in the relevant countries and slightly different regional structures. AHD realized some sales synergies in several countries, in particular in marketing to large hospital groups in recognition of a shift in the health care industry. Hospitals had started to form purchasing consortia to optimize their procurement functions. These purchasing groups were negotiating better deals for the hospitals they represented. To facilitate marketing to these larger hospital groups, the two divisions would jointly serve key accounts, which represented roughly 15 percent of the orthopedics division's sales and 20 percent of the diagnostics division's sales. Mike and Mark were made CEOs of their respective divisions and, like Sergei and Arthur, they remained on the GET.

With the splitting of the international sales force, John's job supervising regional units became largely redundant. John, who was approaching retirement age, asked for "an honorable discharge" from his duties on the GET. He agreed to serve AHD as a senior adviser for another two years before he retired to his ranch in Colorado and embarked on an active second career as a volunteer working with younger veterans.

It took nearly nine months to reorganize AHD and to clarify all the interfaces and interdivisional and intercompany contracts and service level agreements. It was a very demanding project, and many things went wrong on the way, such as the considerable confusion that initially ensued over how to contract services from the GBS division. Some of the services were standardized, but many were not, creating many interface issues between

GBS on one side and AHD's two divisions and Dental Inc. on the other side. Separating Dental Inc. was quite demanding, and several support functions such as finance, human resources, and legal had to be rebuilt within Dental Inc., much to Monica and Vijai's disappointment, since they saw this as a duplication of support functions.

However, the overall effort paid off. When the dust settled, Carl had effectively divided AHD into five smaller real, or notional, companies (Figure 6.8).

The change made accountabilities clear, empowered the management team, and put the five units on an exciting, productive path. The reorganization also improved profitability greatly, silencing those board members (including Fred, the auditor) who had always demanded a major cost-reduction program.

The momentum was strong, and in the summer of 2008 AHD, now called the AHD Group, started to grow rapidly.

The style and culture of the GET also had started to shift. The members' discussions became increasingly focused on content and action. In one of its discussions, the GET reviewed the performance data of five AHD units. The members noticed that after roughly six months, the performance of the five sections had started to vary significantly. Monica's finance department conducted an analysis of the results of the previous six months and found that one unit—Mark's diagnostics business unit—was significantly outperforming all the others.

No apparent differences distinguished the five units of the group. The diagnostics market had the most modest growth, but it was significantly outgrowing the orthopedic implants and dental implants divisions. It was strange that the largest unit, the one in the most difficult market, was outperforming the other two.

Carl decided to spend time with the diagnostics division, trying to understand what made it strong. He could sense that its management team had an enormous sense of passion and energy. The team members talked about patients—the clinic group's customers—all the time. They were completely focused on patients, and talked little about the competition or the market. Interestingly, they didn't seem to be particularly competitive with the other four units of the AHD group, either. It didn't feel as if a desire to appear better than the other units was driving their performance.

One evening Carl went out for a drink with Mark, now CEO of the diagnostics division. Mark had been a creative artist in his youth; today—after a career change, and a successful track record in the orthopedics unit of AHD—he was heading the diagnostics division. Mark was universally

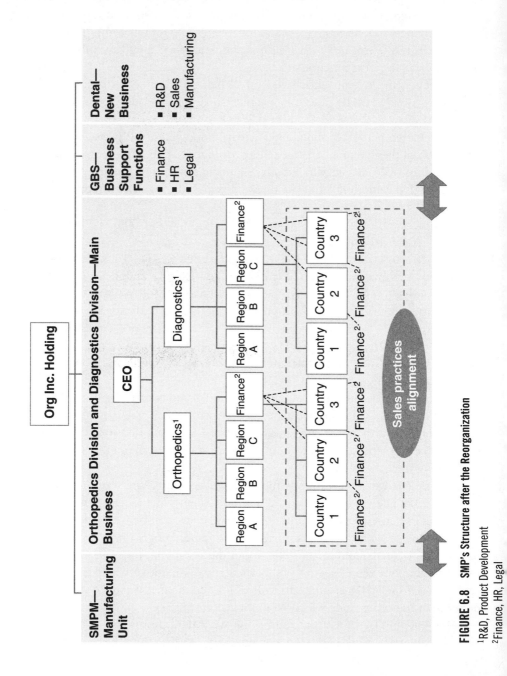

FIGURE 6.8 SMP's Structure after the Reorganization

[1]R&D, Product Development
[2]Finance, HR, Legal

known to be a person with very deep feelings. He was a right-brain type of guy: emotional, devoted, and charismatic. Having stepped away from his former dedication to orthopedics, he was completely committed to diagnostics. The AHD Group saw him as a very inspirational leader. He spoke for hours about the excitement of developing the best possible solutions to help patients live better and longer lives. He lit up with an almost missionary fervor when he discussed how he felt about helping patients.

The secret of the team's success was now one question away, and Carl asked the question: "Mark, why do you feel so strongly about getting the best possible solution for patients?" Mark answered, "My mother died because the gynecologist didn't diagnose her breast cancer early enough. It took two years and two check-ups too many for the doctors to notice that something was wrong. It could have been detected earlier with better solutions. I never, ever, want this to happen again. To anyone."

Mark had a mission. Being at AHD was more than a job for him. It was his opportunity to make a difference in people's lives.

CHAPTER 7

In Brain We Trust

I want to discuss why a company exists in the first place. In other words, why are we here? I think many people assume, wrongly, that a company exists simply to make money. While this is an important result of a company's existence, we have to go deeper and find the real reasons for our being. As we investigate this, we inevitably come to the conclusion that a group of people get together and exist as an institution that we call a company so they are able to accomplish something collectively that they could not accomplish separately—they make a contribution to society, a phrase which sounds trite but is fundamental.

You can look around [in the general business world and] see people who are interested in money and nothing else, but the underlying drives come largely from a desire to do something else: to make a product, to give a service—generally to do something which is of value.

This is part of a speech that Dave Packard gave to Hewlett-Packard employees in 1960 (Collins and Porras 1996). Packard makes the point that people have a desire to do something of value, to fulfill a mission, to give meaning to their lives.

There have been 3,000 years of philosophical debates on the meaning of life, starting with the Greek philosophers—Socrates, Plato, Aristotle, Epicurus, among others—around 600 B.C., and probably even before that; the debate has extended into the present day, with philosophies such as Nihilism (Nietzsche, Camus), Kantism, Pragmatism (James), and Existentialism (Kirkegaard, Sartre).

Religion, a reliable provider of meaning for life, is also highly popular these days. Roughly four out of five of the world's population claim to be religious, to believe in the existence of a god, or gods. Although there is no scientific proof of the existence of a god, of any god, billions of people are members of a religion, perform religious rituals (such as going to services, praying, and so forth), and observe religious values (Tiger and McGuire 2010).

The Roman Catholic Church, for example, has nearly 1.2 billion members, and despite its controversial views on matters such as AIDS, contraception, and abortion, it is a fast-growing institution.

In the nineteenth century, many scientists and philosophers believed that religion was a dying phenomenon. Karl Marx claimed that "religion is the sigh of the oppressed creature, the heart of a heartless world, and the soul of soulless conditions. It is the opium of the people" (Marx 1976).

He and many other philosophers believed that, with the emancipation of the common people, with their access to education, to information, to wealth, the future would be free of religion. They couldn't have been more wrong. Today rich and poor people around the world are religious. The United States, one of the world's richest countries, is also one of the world's most religious ones.

Why do we humans need to have a purpose in life? And why can the existence of something like a firmly held ideology or purpose increase the performance of organizations? We look in this chapter at the concept of the corporate mission or purpose, a concept that can help firms adapt to changes in the environment.

Story-Telling and Spirituality as Neurological Phenomena

In recent years, several neuroscientists have expressed the view that the need and the ability to believe in religion or an ideology is a neurological phenomenon that occurs in our (comparatively oversized) cerebral cortex, much like our abilities for language, music, or planning (Bolte Taylor 2008; Linden 2010; Tiger and McGuire 2010).

David Linden, professor of neurosciences at John Hopkins University in Baltimore, believes that our brain has a story-telling instinct, located in the left side of the cerebral cortex, that develops stories out of seemingly unrelated matters in order to produce coherent and logical explanations. Observations are transformed into coherent stories that can build a bridge between those observations that we can explain and those that we cannot (Linden 2010).

This instinct, to develop coherent stories in the left side of the cerebral cortex, has been well researched with a group of split-brain patients. Split-brain patients are those in whom the connection between the two brain hemispheres (known as the corpus callosum) has been partially or fully severed. Severing this connection is often the ultimate, but effective, measure for treating patients with specific forms of epilepsy, so as to avoid accidental physical injury during epileptic seizures. Split-brain patients have normal brain activity and function, with the difference that the left and right sides of their cortex perform their work independently. This enables us to observe the functions of the two halves of the cortex separately.

The analysis of split-brain patients goes back to the 1950s and the work of Roger Sperry of the California Institute of Technology. Sperry was a neurobiologist who won the Nobel Prize for Medicine in 1981 for his work with split-brain patients, and his work has spurred intense research on cerebral hemispheres (Linden 2010).

With most people, the left side of the cortex specializes in complex cognitive processes such as mathematical calculations or language. The left side of the cortex is able to perform other functions such as associating facts to build stories and develop conceptions of the future (planning). By contrast, the right side of the cortex is directly involved with spatial thinking, recognition of faces, and the sensation of emotions embedded in language, music, or mimicry. The right side is usually concerned with the present, with the now (Bolte Taylor 2008; Linden 2010).

In a well-known experiment by Michael Gazzaniga, a student of Sperry's and professor of psychology at the University of California, Santa Barbara, illustrated in his book *The Mind's Past,* split-brain patients were put in front of a screen so that visual stimuli reaching the right and left side of their cortexes corresponded to different pictures. The left hemisphere was shown a picture of a chicken claw (through the right eye, as the left cortex controls the right side of the body and vice versa) and the right hemisphere one of winter scenery. When asked to select a card that would fit to the picture shown on the screen, the right hand (controlled by the left side of the cortex) selected a picture of a chicken, while the left hand (controlled by the right side of the cortex) selected a shovel, which suited the snowy countryside shown on the screen. When patients were asked why they had chosen the shovel, the left-side (only the left side can speak) answer was: "Well, that's easy. The claw fits the chicken, and you need a shovel to clean out the henhouse." The left-side cortex saw the claw but not the winter countryside, but it invented a coherent story to explain why it chose the shovel. The left-side cortex could have said, "I have no idea, why do you ask?" but it didn't (Gazzaniga 1998; Linden 2010).

Beyond the story-telling instinct of our brain, a second factor seems to influence its religious and spiritual instinct: the spiritual predisposition of the right side of the cortex. As we learned earlier, the right side is more predisposed to sensing and feeling emotions, and to spatial orientation.

In her account of the consequences of a stroke that severely damaged her brain's left side, neuroanatomist Dr. Jill Bolte Taylor describes her own sensations on the morning of the stroke: "As the language centers in my left hemisphere grew increasingly silent and I became detached from the memories of my life, I was comforted by an expanding sense of grace. In this void of higher cognition and details pertaining to my normal life, my consciousness soared into an all-knowingness, a 'being at home' with the universe, if you will. In a compelling sort of way, it felt like the good road home, and I liked it. By this point, I had lost touch with much of the physical three-dimensional reality that surrounded me. My body was propped up against the shower wall and I found it odd that I was aware that I could no longer clearly discern the physical boundaries of where I began and where I ended. I sensed the composition of my being as that of a fluid rather than that of a solid. I no longer perceived myself as a whole object separate from everything" (Bolte Taylor 2008).

Her experience seems to be confirmed by the work of Andrew Newberg, associate professor of radiology and psychiatry in the School of Medicine at the University of Pennsylvania, and Eugene D'Aquili, a research psychiatrist, who invited Tibetan monks and Franciscan nuns to meditate or pray inside a SPECT machine (single photon emission computed tomography), which enables brain activity to be imaged. The experiments identified shifts in mental activity during phases of deep meditation or prayer in a specific area of the brain, including a reduced activity within the language and logical centers of the left cortex, as a reduced activity in the posterior parietal gyrus (the ridge or fold between two clefts on the cerebral surface in the brain) of the left hemisphere, which is believed to help us identify our physical boundaries (Newberg, D'Aquili, and Rause 2001). When this area is inhibited, we lose sight of where our body begins and where we end relative to the space around us, generating a feeling that we are *one* with the universe around us (Bolte Taylor 2008).

Most of us are not split-brain patients, so we combine the predisposition to make sense of the unknown (left hemisphere) and the predisposition to spirituality (right hemisphere). But why do we use these predispositions to develop religion? And how do they shape our drive and sense of purpose in business?

Why Our Brain Develops Religion

In their book *God's Brain,* Lionel Tiger, anthropologist and Charles Darwin professor of anthropology at Rutgers University, and neuroscientist Michael McGuire, try to answer these questions.

They believe that there are several reasons for the development of religion. Let's explore three: Religion provides clarity in answering the question "What for?"; religion satisfies an innate human egalitarian bias; and religion provides identity, the feeling of being one of the chosen, being something special (Somm 2010; Tiger and McGuire 2010).

The first reason has to do with our huge cerebral cortex enabling us to imagine future situations, to plan. Other mammals are believed to live only in the present, while humans can think about the future. This ability allows us to develop long-term strategies, and make decisions today that will have effects in the future (like sowing grain today and harvesting it months later). Tiger and McGuire believe that this predisposition also creates significant stress and anxiety: anxiety about death, anxiety about the vagueness of our lives. They believe that this is less a fear of death, but rather a matter of "What for?" or "What is the purpose of all this?" They believe that religion is a human creation capable of soothing this anxiety.

People who consider themselves religious report living happier lives (and philosophers are more prone to depression). People who regularly perform religious rituals such as praying or going to church produce a measurably higher level of serotonin (the happiness hormone) in their brains. To cope with the stress and anxiety of our lives, our brain needs to see a purpose, a meaning for our actions (Somm 2010; Tiger and McGuire 2010).

The second reason has to do with what anthropologists call the *egalitarian bias*. Anthropologists believe that humans have an innate need for justice, for being treated equally, and for helping less fortunate people. However, life isn't fair or just. Some people are born rich, some poor. Some become rich by cheating, or at least displaying questionable ethical behavior. Some are born ugly, others good looking. Some have successful careers, others don't. Some are more fortunate in their life, and live a long and healthy life. Some die early, too early.

But before God at least, we believe we are all equal. There are no bosses, no subordinates, there are no rich and no poor, there are no good-looking or ugly souls in paradise. Only the souls of people who live a just life (however that is defined, for there are more than 4,200 religions in the world) are likely to enter paradise, or wherever the good go (Somm 2010; Tiger and McGuire 2010).

The third reason seems to have to do with every religion offering human beings a sense of being unique, one of the chosen, someone special, which is obviously quite motivating (but also creates a not inconsiderable social and political problem, in that each religion believes it is the only true one) (Somm 2010).

Religion is on the rise in the world. Robert William Fogel, a Nobel laureate in economics, writes in his book *The Fourth Great Awakening and the Future of Egalitarism* that "spiritual inequity is today as big a problem as material inequity" (Fogel 2000). Viktor Frankl, a neurologist and psychiatrist as well as a Nazi concentration camp survivor, wrote: "People have enough to live, but nothing to live for; they have the means but not the meaning" (Frankl 1984).

If spirituality is an innate neurological need, and that need is growing, what are the implications for business?

Unleashing Spirituality in Business

In their report, *A Spiritual Audit of Corporate America,* Ian Mitroff, a professor at the University of Southern California, and Elizabeth A. Denton, an organizational consultant, write that employees hunger to bring their spiritual values, their whole person, and not just their (left) brain to work. They also found that companies that acknowledged spiritual values and that aligned them with corporate ones, outperformed companies that didn't (Mitroff and Denton 1999).

In their influential book *Built to Last,* Jim Collins and Jerry Porras, write that companies built to last, firms that have shaped industries for decades, have a well-articulated corporate ideology (which includes a core purpose statement and a statement of "what we stand for") that is present and pervasive in their everyday work (Collins and Porras 1994).

If talented people want to do something with their lives, today's global labor markets offer them, maybe more than ever, opportunities to do so. They can work for companies; they can work for NGOs; they can work for international not-for-profit institutions. More than ever, firms need to really put their mission statements into practice if they are to attract, develop, and retain exceptional people.

A company ideology should first and foremost be *authentic;* that means it should be meaningful (meaning-full) to the firm leadership. An ideology that is *authentic,* and genuinely put into practice can be a unique asset for a firm because it may address a neurological demand, satisfy an innate need that people have, and provide a source of identification for the organization's members. It may generate in them a commitment to beliefs and values that are greater than themselves (Mgbere 2009). It may also establish the potential to elicit strong emotions (and amygdala involvement) in others outside the organization, which may make them perceive it as unique (and want to join it).

Yet despite significant evidence of its importance, many leaders feel uncomfortable talking of meaning in the workplace. Concerns that they may nurture cynicism among employees, that they may be perceived as manipulative, or that they may be seen as preaching and dogmatizing (especially in secular Europe) make them hesitant in addressing meaning in the workplace.

This is probably part of the reason why the mission statements and values posters in many firms aren't worth the paper they are printed on. More often than not, they exist because managers believe that having such statements is part of good management. After all, most management books talk about them, so it probably makes good sense to have them, too.

Ultimately, it is a matter of personal choice and belief how intensely a leader wants to work with ideology and meaning in the workplace, how much energy he or she wants to devote to articulating, preaching, and living the corporate ideology. The available research does, however, indicate that this is an area that deserves consideration.

Insights on Company Ideologies

Whatever importance leaders assign to the topic, there are a few insights that may be helpful. Corporate ideologies are probably more effective when they meet three criteria: they are altruistic, they are told through stories and metaphors, and the organization is visibly committed to them.

Altruistic

Firms can have very different *raisons d'être,* very different missions or purposes. Some firms focus on becoming or being the most respected, successful organization in an industry, and their statements typically read like this:

"Our mission is to be the most respected company in our industry."
"Our mission is to be the company most admired for its people and performance."
"Our mission is to operate the best retail business."

Other firms define outcomes as their company purpose, and their mission statements typically read like this:

"The purpose of our company is to earn money for the shareholders and increase the value of their investment."
"Our mission is to grow profitably."

Finally, some firms define their mission as serving customers and helping people. Their mission statements tend to read as follows:

"Our mission is to improve patients' lives."
"Our purpose is to promote the financial well-being of our customers and their families."
"Our mission is to provide the best possible service to our guests around the world."

Insights from psychology and anthropology suggest that people have an altruistic bias, an innate need to help and support others, especially if these others are less healthy, as is the case for patients, or less fortunate in life.

We may hypothesize that mission statements focused on helping others are powerful in providing meaning to members of organizations. For example, most statements of the core purpose of firms cited in *Built to Last* are focused on helping customers (Table 7.1).

Stories and Metaphors

Company mission statements are likely to be more powerful when brought alive with inspiring stories and metaphors. Mission statements are often composed of a list of generic phrases. However, our brain has difficulty memorizing lists and blank statements. It can handle stories and metaphors much better. "Narrative imaging—stories—is the fundamental instrument of

TABLE 7.1   Examples of Core Purpose

Company	Core Purpose
3M	To solve unsolved problems innovatively
Cargill	To improve the standard of living around the world
Fannie Mae	To strengthen the social fabric by continually democratizing home ownership
Hewlett-Packard	To make technical contributions for the advancement and welfare of humanity
Israel	To provide a secure place on Earth for the Jewish people
Lost Arrow Corporation	To be a role model and tool for social change
Pacific Theatres	To provide a place for people to flourish and to enhance the community
Mary Kay	To give unlimited opportunity to women
McKinsey	To help leading corporations and governments be more successful
Merck	To preserve and improve human life
Nike	To experience the emotion of competition, winning, and crushing competitors
Sony	To experience the joy of advancing and applying technology for the benefit of the public
Telecare	To help people with mental impairments realize their full potential
Wal-Mart	To give ordinary folk the chance to buy the same things as rich people
Disney	To make people happy

Source: Collins, J., and J. I. Porras. "Building Your Company's Vision." *Harvard Business Review* 68 (1996): 65–77. Reprinted with permission.

our thought," writes neuroscientist Mark Turner in *The Library Mind*. Most of our thinking, our experience, our knowledge, is organized as stories (Turner 2006).

Hollywood and Bollywood tell us stories. The Bible is a story. And it is no coincidence that some of the best leaders in history have been great, inspirational storytellers, using metaphors and positive visions. John F. Kennedy and Winston Churchill, for example, come to mind (Deutschman 2005).

Stories and metaphors illustrating companies' missions may need to be told frequently, repeatedly, and in a positive context. As we have seen in the chapter on the wired brain, repetition (consolidation) and positive framing are important factors that help people memorize concepts, internalize values, and ultimately, change their behavior.

Visible Commitments

Company ideologies and mission statements will be more powerful when the organization is visibly committed to them. Commitment means that the organization is willing to devote precious time, to spend money, and to incur financial losses or to forgo gains in adhering to its mission or purpose.

For example, in 2009, Novartis, a Swiss pharmaceutical company, contributed $1.5 billion, or more than 3 percent of its revenue, and significant management time to various not-for-profit initiatives to help patients—from funding drug donations and research programs to combating neglected diseases like malaria, tuberculosis, and leprosy in developing nations, to supporting patient assistance programs that help cancer patients receive the most effective treatments available. In doing so, it helped improve the lives of nearly 80 million patients, who could not afford to pay for expensive drugs and who would otherwise not have received much help.

Novartis also finances and organizes an annual Community Partnership Day: Every year more than 10,000 employees worldwide engage in volunteer work for a wide range of charitable causes such as accompanying elderly people on excursions, gardening with handicapped people, working with schools for children with AIDS, maintaining emergency rooms in public hospitals, reconditioning orphanages, or collecting winter coats for homeless people and business clothing for low-income women seeking to reenter the workforce.

■ ■ ■

It was an established reality: Carl had cancer. Having cancer should have felt agonizing and depressing, but oddly it didn't. He was surprised about it and—despite diagnosis and treatment—felt serene and at peace with his life.

During one chemo infusion, he had a conversation with a young man who was receiving palliative cancer treatment, and who would live for only another year. The man was calm and deeply grateful for the time he had been given to close down his life in an orderly fashion, and to say goodbye to all those whom he loved. "Many people die suddenly in an accident and don't get this precious time to say goodbye," Carl remembered him saying. This captured Carl's feelings well. Carl was grateful for the time he still had.

But he was also grateful for the life he had already lived, a life that hadn't started well.

He had lost his parents when he was four years old. Growing up in an orphanage, he developed a ridiculously ambitious and competitive character, and with it some edgy and destructive behavior. Behavior that he was forced to change—as a direct result of having been twice expelled from school because of his own actions—becoming more unassuming, more collaborative, and soft-spoken as he matured.

As he grew up, he learned to control his emotions better, graduated from a second-league college, and went on to have a great career that eventually led to KenkoInc and then to his appointment as AHD's president and CEO.

Part of Carl's change was due to his family, to Gwen in particular. He had met Gwen toward the end of his time at college. She knew how to speak to his emotions, and how to bring out the good part in him, as she would say.

They married soon after graduation, and were delighted when Dave and Alex came along. Brown-haired, brown-eyed and athletic like their mother, the children were smart, well mannered, and well liked. Carl and Gwen were very proud of them.

Carl not only felt serene and at peace with his life, he also felt that he was living his life more intensely. He became more conscious of the value of time, and keen to always do the right thing, as he felt he would have little time to go back to correct flawed decisions and actions. Also, he felt able to sense and savor more of the world around him than ever before—the color of the sky on a long and warm summer evening, the way the pine trees smelled when he was walking in the forest, the feelings of people around him.

For example, he was able to relate to Mark's feelings in a way that was new to him. The tragic story of Mark's mother dying of a misdiagnosis had given Mark a mission, a purpose in life: to ensure that AHD would sell diagnostic solutions enabling doctors to diagnose cancer early, when it could often still be treated and cured effectively. It was a positive mission, helping cancer patients around the world.

AHD already had a mission statement. It read: "Helping patients live better and longer lives." But Carl didn't think the mission statement seemed to matter much either to the board, or to the management team.

He realized that no one on the board or in the GET ever talked about patients. All they discussed were business matters such as changes in the share price, the latest technologies, how their competitors were doing, financial reports, organizational issues, the corporate citizenship program, and so forth. He hadn't heard any discussion about what the company ultimately existed to do: help patients.

How could the board or the top team expect the entire organization to be passionate about helping patients, as Mark was, if that goal meant so little to its leaders?

For Carl, the situation was different. Carl was a cancer patient. Chemotherapy was keeping him alive. He felt deeply grateful for the years he could still live. He knew that it was people—the scientists, managers, and employees at pharmaceutical firms—who had persevered, worked hard, developed, and brought to the market medicines that were keeping him alive. A patient himself, he believed in, and was passionate about, AHD's noble mission of helping people to live longer lives.

But he needed to ignite the same passion with the board and his top team.

In early 2007, he proposed to the board that each director would visit patients, not customers—physicians, clinics, and hospitals—but patients whose cancer was detected early, patients who had received implants and could now live better, healthier lives.

Carl also introduced an annual "Patient Day," during which he expected his top 50 people, including the top management team, to go into clinics and hospitals and talk to patients. He wanted them to experience the emotions of the men, women, and children that AHD had helped.

As the head of the company, Carl also often received letters from patients who had benefited from AHD Group's products. These were warm-hearted, inspiring letters from people who were deeply grateful for what AHD had done for them. Carl decided to send some of these letters, after deleting the patients' names, to the board, the GET, and his top 50 people.

The visits, the Patient Day, and the letters hit the mark. The board members and the top 50 executives carried *stories* into the organizations, stories of people who could walk again after receiving artificial joints, of women whose cancer had been detected early and who could now see their grandchildren grow up, of people who could again play sports after having received artificial hip implants.

The organization was flooded with stories of how AHD had helped save and improve patients' lives. This created enormous energy, passion, and momentum.

Carl was satisfied. The organization had internalized the OPEN strategy, and the reassertion of AHD's mission had recharged the broader organization. The company was doing increasingly well.

However, the situation was about to be spoiled by a very fundamental change in the environment. Following a banking crisis in the United States that quickly affected the European banking system (Reinhart and Rogoff 2009), and had reached its (emotional) climax with the bankruptcy of Lehman Brothers in September 2008, the global economy headed toward a deep recession—the deepest the world had experienced since before the Second World War.

Central banks and governments around the world poured huge sums into their nations' economies in an attempt to stabilize the global banking system and to keep their economies going. Despite these enormous—and historically unprecedented—interventions, the global economy spiraled downward.

By the end of 2008, GDP was falling in most of the economies that were important for the AHD Group, including the United States, Germany, the UK, France, Italy, and Spain. On the other hand, the emerging market economies were doing relatively well, but this was of little value to AHD, given its limited presence in those markets.

The AHD Group's customers were very nervous. Many hospitals and clinics postponed their investments in diagnostic equipment and used up their inventories of consumables.

In late 2008, AHD's largest Japanese competitor, InVit, took over VisioMed, another major AHD rival. Because of significant overlaps between VisioMed and InVit in their sales infrastructure and production systems, a wave of layoffs followed the takeover.

This provoked a great deal of anxiety among AHD's employees. Many were deeply troubled about the developments in the industry, and the takeover and layoffs at VisioMed were a serious source of worry for most of them.

Carl was very concerned. He was worried that the recession would spoil all of his and the GET's efforts to turn AHD around, since the company's improved position and momentum were still fragile.

He was afraid that the organization was not yet ready to withstand the crisis that was unfolding.

CHAPTER 8

What We Value

A key finding of both the Australian Prudential Regulation Authority report and a controversial PricewaterhouseCoopers investigation into the currency losses was the need for sweeping changes to the bank's culture.

It was described as being too bureaucratic and focused on process and documentation, rather than understanding the substance of issues, "taking responsibility and resolving the matters."

All levels of management were criticized for encouraging a "good-news culture" that cocooned top decision-makers from information that might have enabled the bank to avoid a string of corporate mishaps, ranging from the $3.5 billion HomeSide losses to the currency scandal.

This passage is taken from an article that appeared in the *Sydney Morning Herald*, which investigated the losses that occurred at the National Australia Bank in 1990s (Hughes 2004; Stanford 2007). As the example shows, companies can develop highly dysfunctional cultures. As a result, these firms may miss changes in the environment, they may perpetuate ingrained habits, and they may find it more difficult to adapt. Organizational cultures that no longer fit the environment can become tremendous stumbling blocks that impede change (Mgbere 2009).

An organization may have dysfunctional values. Perhaps a CEO has led a firm through a deep and difficult crisis that has threatened the existence of the organization, a very emotional and difficult moment for its members. He or she has done so very successfully, by taking an "executing and working harder" approach that has mutated into a tacit assumption and become reality in the form of artifacts ("stories of how we succeeded," values statements stressing the need for getting things done), values, and norms (for example, meetings that are brief and focus on execution, and faster promotions for people who get things done).

Then just as the crisis is overcome, what if the company suddenly faces a tectonic change in its industry that can be mastered successfully only with an entirely different approach, one that stresses exploration, collaboration, and creativity? In such a situation, an organizational culture generally runs on autopilot and continues to reinforce a set of individual behaviors and corporate reactions that are out of date and ineffective in the new context.

This is even more dangerous when the organizational culture is established, strong, and dominant. In this case, there is a risk that it will suppress other perspectives and the opinions of new members of the organization, who may not share the current culture's tacit assumptions and values. By suppressing subcultures that could be helpful, a dominant culture limits the articulation of different values that could help an organization manage crises and change (Mgbere 2009).

Organizational culture can be an important stumbling block, so—since we have already examined organizational bureaucracy and lack of a coherent organizational mission—this is the third factor of organizational rigidity that we will study.

Understanding Corporate Culture

The notion of corporate culture is relatively new, and academics and managers frequently disagree about what organizational culture is, and to what extent it can be managed (Bandura 1997; Harder 1999). It is a difficult concept to grasp, to measure, and to explain, yet most managers believe intuitively that it is important, and the management of corporate culture belongs today among the standard repertoire of a CEO's interventions.

Culture as a concept is largely a matter of sociology and anthropology, where it is well researched as a set of values and norms of groups of individuals.

Some of the first mentions of the term *organizational* or *corporate* culture are to be found in the early 1980s, in books such as *In Search of Excellence* (Peters and Waterman 1982), or *Theory Z* (Ouchi 1981).

One of the most distinguished thinkers and academics in the area of organizational culture is Edgar Henry Schein, a professor at MIT. He is generally credited with creating the term *corporate culture.*

Schein defines corporate culture as: "The pattern of basic assumptions that a given group has invented, discovered, or developed in learning to cope with its problems of external adaption and internal integration, and that have worked well enough to be considered valid, and therefore, to be taught to new members as the correct way they perceive, think, and feel in relation to these problems" (Schein 1985).

He describes corporate culture at three levels.

At the first level are organizational attributes that the uninitiated observer can see, feel, and hear. Schein calls them artifacts. Artifacts are cultural symbols of various types, and could include stories that are told about the organization's history, rituals, or ceremonies (for example, choreography and speeches given by senior organizational members at on-boarding events or retirement dinners), and physical settings (for example, layout or architectural features). As an example, at Nike, an American athletic apparel firm (the ones that can "just do it"), executives serve as corporate storytellers, explicitly connecting the company's values to its heritage through motivating stories about how the company was founded.

The next level deals with the values ("we value punctuality") and norms ("one should not be late") of an organization. Schein calls this level the professed culture. Values and norms can be seen in a company's policies and procedures manuals, recruiting and on-boarding processes, performance management (appraisal and reward) systems, promotion guidelines, signature authority, interaction styles, and patterns about which rules to follow and which to ignore. In essence, the professed culture consists of visible expressions of "what we value around here."

At the third and deepest level of a corporate culture are the organization's tacit assumptions. These are the elements of culture that are not observable in everyday work. Some of these may be elements of culture that are taboo to discuss. Many of these unwritten rules exist without the conscious knowledge of the organizations' members. Those with sufficient experience to understand this deepest level of organizational culture usually become acclimatized to its attributes over time.

Schein's model helps us understand paradoxical organizational behaviors. For example, an organization can stress moral standards at the second level of Schein's model while simultaneously displaying opposing behavior at the third and deepest level of its culture. This helps to explain the difficulties that an organization's newcomers have in assimilating its corporate culture and why it takes time to become an insider. It also explains why leaders sometimes fail to achieve their goals: They do not really understand the underlying tacit cultural norms of their organization before they try to change its culture.

Subcultures

Much of what we have been discussing so far concerns the dominant or main culture of an organization (if it has one). But any group of individuals in an organization can form a subculture. Subcultures may originate from departmental or divisional memberships, from occupational or professional affiliations, or from national or regional differences, and can be categorized into three types: enhancing, complementary, and counterculture (Harder 1999).

An *enhancing subculture* holds the same tacit assumptions as the main culture, but holds them even more intensively. One example is Apple, which is known for its innovative products, including the Macintosh computer, the iMac, the iPod, the iPhone, and the iPad. In the 1980s, the stereotype of Apple was that it was filled with anti-establishment, rule-breaking innovators, people who wanted something better than Microsoft's operating system. The Macintosh unit was even more aggressive in its push to reinvent the personal computer industry. This didn't conflict with the main culture, but was a subculture (Harder 1999).

A *complementary subculture* builds on the same tacit assumptions as the main culture, and additionally on some other nonconflicting assumptions. One example might be the finance department in a corporation, in which the main assumptions are held, plus assumptions particular to the finance profession (Harder 1999).

A *counterculture* builds on some assumptions that conflict with the tacit assumptions of the main culture. John DeLorean's group at General Motors was an example of a counterculture. DeLorean was a capable young engineer and innovator, and the youngest person to ever become a General Motors executive. While General Motors as a whole was very status-conscious, DeLorean's team was the antithesis (Harder 1999). Tired of frictions with General Motors's main culture, DeLorean departed in 1975 to set up his own company, the DeLorean Motor Company. The company produced the stainless steel DeLorean DMC-12 sports car, which achieved fame in the *Back to the Future* movie trilogy.

Using Culture to Reduce Need for Deep and Dense Hierarchies

Organizational culture can be powerful in complementing a company's formal structure and in reducing the need for extensive, complex hierarchies and processes. Culture can help guide the daily activities of employees and their decision making in the absence of written rules or policies (Mallak 2001). It enables greater decentralization of power and adaptation to the demands of specific situations. Cultural rules provide general guidance but leave the specific way how up to the individual, allowing more space for adaptation at the front line.

In doing so, culture replaces detailed process and job descriptions—what we described earlier as *ossification*—with values and norms that provide general guidelines that employees can use to interpret facts and decide on courses of action in new, unknown situations.

Successful adaptive organizations tend to make more use of values and cultural norms that foster collaboration, teamwork, and innovation to counteract the inherent rigidities of the deep and dense hierarchies and processes (Beinhocker 2006; Daft 2007).

Execution and Learning Culture

In recent years, numerous studies and books have discussed building so-called learning or adaptive corporate cultures. The authors often argue that organizations need to create the environment for people to exchange perspectives, to debate matters, to learn, and progress. While this sounds noble, organizations are essentially set up to implement and execute strategies and business plans.

Eric Beinhocker, an economist and the author of *The Origin of Wealth,* takes a more nuanced view and believes that a good culture is able to combine these two elements (Beinhocker 2006).

First, the tacit assumptions, values, and norms need to facilitate execution of the current strategy. A good culture contains a strong element of getting things done. High performance cultures include, among other elements, strategy execution and organizational unity (Klein 2008). Beinhocker calls these norms *performing and collaborating norms.*

Second, a good culture contains elements that foster learning and adaptation, and that facilitate change. A culture that embodies flexibility and openness to new ideas and styles sets the stage for a change-oriented organization and helps employees cope with the tensions associated with change (Recardo, Molloy, and Pellegrino 1995). Values and norms of countercultures can be useful in providing openness, in raising issues that would not be addressed within the dominant culture, and are necessary for organizational success or survival (Hardy 1999). Beinhocker calls these *innovating norms.*

In his study, Beinhocker portrayed a good culture with 10 norms, which he calls "The Ten Commandments" (Beinhocker 2006). They are set out here:

Performing Norms

1. Performance orientation: Always do your best, go the extra mile, take initiative, and continuously improve yourself.
2. Honesty: Be honest with others, be honest with yourself, be transparent and face reality.
3. Meritocracy: Reward people on the basis of merit.

Cooperating Norms

4. Mutual trust: Trust your colleagues' motivation, and trust their skills to get the job done.
5. Reciprocity: Live the Golden Rule: Do unto others as you would have them do unto you.
6. Shared purpose: Put the organization's interest ahead of your own, and behave as if everyone is in it together.

Innovating Norms

7. Nonhierarchical: Junior people are expected to challenge senior people, and what matters is the quality of an idea, not the title of the person saying it.
8. Openness: Be curious, open to outside thinking, and willing to experiment. Seek the best wherever it is.
9. Fact-based: Find out the facts. It is fact, not opinions, that ultimately count.
10. Challenge: Feel a sense of competitive urgency. It is a race without a finishing line.

Transforming Culture

Changing a culture is a matter of leadership, and the most effective and efficient architect of the culture is the most senior leader of the organization, typically the CEO. Schein argues that leadership is the creation, management, and at times the destruction and reconstruction of culture (Schein 1985). In fact, he goes as far as to say that the "only thing of importance that leaders do is to create and manage culture."

The CEO changes the culture by applying and embedding new tacit assumptions and core beliefs (level three) into the values and norms of the culture, the artifacts, and the professed culture (levels one and two).

The CEO uses effective behavior (role modeling) and communication (language, storytelling) to change and embed culture. Jan Carlzon's behavior during the turnaround of SAS, a Scandinavian airline, in the 1990s is a good example of the former. Carlzon believed that increasing flight punctuality was the key to turning SAS around. He therefore regularly monitored flight punctuality in real time, from a terminal in his office. He used to call the gates directly to inquire about reasons for late departures.

Medtronic, a U.S. medical device firm, offers an example of storytelling. At Medtronic, new employees participate in two-hour "mission and medallion sessions" with top executives, to hear stories that illustrate the importance of the company's values and specific examples of how individual employees contribute; the medallion featuring the corporate symbol is personally presented to each employee by the CEO or other senior executives at meetings held throughout the world.

Furthermore, culture is changed by means of interventions in formal mechanisms that embody values and norms such as making changes to the recruiting and on-boarding processes, adapting incentive schemes, or changing the appraisal and reward process.

Cultural change efforts are typically most effective in situations of crisis, or when the leader changes. The members of the organization are then insecure, and their attention to changes is heightened. They are sensitive to ongoing changes, including subtle ones.

Importantly, and building on what we learned in previous chapters, leaders should frame the change story positively to reduce individual stress and anxiety, and to create the preconditions for creativity, learning, and change.

■ ■ ■

"We need to prepare for the worst," Monica, the CFO, proclaimed at the GET meeting, sounding even more urgent than usual. "We need to reduce our investment in building our positions in the emerging markets, and we need to cut costs to protect our margins."

The benefits of the reorganization had not yet fully kicked in, and Monica was concerned that a potential sales slowdown would hurt margins and consume AHD's limited reserves.

Monica continued: "First, we should stop our investments in China, India, and Brazil. That would be only prudent. We need to protect our liquidity. Second, I propose introducing a hiring freeze and reducing our staff by 15 percent across the board. Personnel costs are our most important cost block; we need to address it. Third, we should reduce sourced costs, taking advantage of the crisis. Many suppliers are struggling. We should leverage this for better sourcing deals."

"What about manufacturing?" objected the ever-practical Arthur, more focused on production than ever as head of AHDM. "A 15 percent reduction in staff? We can't do that, at least not in manufacturing. I am fully aware of the budgetary issues, but we would endanger our ability to deliver the products to our customers on time. I am also skeptical about sourcing. Our product quality still needs to improve, and I do not want to go back to where we were just a few years ago."

"I agree—15 percent is not feasible. Dental implants sales are still growing. I can't cut staff," said Sergei worriedly, as Mike and Mark concurred. Their units were also still growing and they, too, resisted the idea of staff cuts.

Vijai, the head of GBS, said, "I could try to accelerate the offshoring of activities to our center in India, and I could speak to a few outsourcing partners. Maybe we could reduce costs in back-office functions more quickly than we had planned."

Carl had listened carefully. "Let's agree on a few principles before we discuss measures. In my mind, there are four. First, we will not do anything that endangers our ability to provide our customers with high quality products. Second, we will not fire any employees, unless—as the last resort—we are forced to do so to prevent the company from going bankrupt. Our employees have committed to us. We have to commit to them, even if this reduces our profitability in the short term. Third, we will reduce costs where we can, but in line with the first two principles. For example, I believe that we can reduce our sourcing costs, that we can reduce our travel expenses, that we can cut company events and sponsoring, and that we can be more frugal in various other areas. Fourth, we will take a prudent stance on investments. What do you guys think?"

"But, Carl, if we don't reduce staff, our profit margin may go down," Monica said, consciously trying to mitigate her usual abruptness but, as always, focused on the bottom line.

"I know, Monica. It may. But we can't be the 'OPEN employer,' meaning a great employer, only in good times. I am willing to run the risk of decreasing profit margins—to an extent. Should that happen, I am willing to take the heat from the shareholders. Back to the four principles, do we all agree?" said Carl.

The members of the GET agreed, passing a specific plan that included:

- An acceleration of the offshoring and outsourcing measures, combined with a hiring freeze in the GBS unit.
- A sourcing program (with strong quality requirements from AHDM).
- A change to the travel policy, requesting that employees travel in economy.
- A very frugal approach to events and expenses in other areas.

Carl then told all the members of the GET that it was essential for the credibility of the plan that they all (including Carl) walked the talk. He asked them to comply visibly with the new travel policy and to exemplify frugality wherever they could. He asked them to be good role models.

Carl and his GET colleagues spent a lot of time communicating with leaders throughout the organization about the situation and about the measures they were taking, and about AHD's approach toward customers and employees, and toward costs. To engage employees, they asked the workforce to contribute ideas to the approach the GET had put forward. They asked the workforce to stay focused on executing the strategy, to collaborate in bringing the best products to the customers, and to cooperate in finding opportunities for further cost savings.

The key message sent out by Carl and the GET was simple. "We are in this together. Let's work hard and work together to get through this situation."

To keep everyone in the organization updated on the company's progress as the crisis unfolded, Carl and his colleagues organized regular monthly town hall–like meetings. This helped them achieve companywide transparency on how AHD was navigating through the crisis.

AHD was navigating well, very well, in fact.

The open architecture OPEN strategy was working. AHD had clearly the best offerings in orthopedic implants, dental implants, and diagnostics. While the market was contracting, AHD Group's sales were growing.

As sales growth accelerated, and as the effect of the cost measures started to kick in, the profit margins exploded. It was impressive. The mood started to shift, and anxiety slowly vanished. The organization felt more and more confident, more and more like a winner!

But increased sales marked more than just business success. The organization had mastered a crisis with a new approach, an approach focused on both execution and collaboration to bring the best products to AHD customers. During the crisis, the employees had started to reach out of their own sections of the organization and to collaborate in bringing the best possible offerings to the customers. A culture that combined execution and collaboration began to emerge throughout AHD.

Carl and the GET wanted to anchor the emerging culture through the use of *incentives* that would nurture collaboration as much as execution. They told the board that they needed to change the incentive scheme, and to introduce—in addition to rewards for achieving divisional and unit targets—monetary incentives to foster collaboration. Fred, the auditor, and Martin, the investment banker, were vocally on their side this time, so it wasn't very difficult to persuade the rest of the board. Under Monica's careful financial monitoring, AHD soon launched a new incentive scheme.

The incentives were specific. For example, someone who generated a so-called warm lead (identifying a customer who was interested in buying products from another division) would be rewarded with $1,000. A person who promoted contract manufacturing services to third parties would receive $500. AHD also introduced penalties for acts of noncollaboration. For example, people would be fined $250 if they skipped a key-account process meeting or a cross-divisional event. The GET particularly emphasized the yearly regional retreats, at which AHD Group's top 100 regional executives met for their traditional professional leadership weekend.

This sophisticated incentive scheme, with its catalogue of rewards and fines, seemed to work well, at least at the start—but something about it made Carl uncomfortable. Mark didn't like it, either: "For a while, our people were cooperating to help the company out of a jam, to help patients," he told Carl. "Now they are just counting awards."

After a while, Carl and Mark's other colleagues on the management team began to concur. They had a distinct feeling that people had started to take action only if they were paid to do so. Somehow, Carl felt that AHD was starting to depart from its patient-focused mindset: Everybody was talking about money, and how to make more of it.

One day over lunch, Carl shared this feeling and these observations with Felix, an old friend from college. Felix was now a renowned psychologist, and a professor in the psychology department of Cornell University. "Felix, these people are making a lot of money, and more since the introduction of incentives to foster collaboration. But collaboration, real collaboration, is still rare. How the hell do you explain that?" Carl asked.

Felix's answer was insightful.

CHAPTER 9

What Not to Pay For

Imagine for a moment that you are the manager of a day care center. You have a clearly stated policy that children are supposed to be picked up at 4 P.M. But parents are often late. The result: At the end of the day, you have some anxious children and at least one teacher who must wait around for the parents to arrive. What to do? A pair of economists who had heard of this dilemma—it turned out to be a rather common one—offered a solution: Fine the parents who are late. Why, after all, should the day care center take care of these kids for free?

The economists decided to test their solution by conducting a study of 10 day care centers in Haifa, Israel. The study lasted 20 weeks, but the fine was not introduced immediately. For the first four weeks, the economists simply kept track of the number of parents who came late; there were, on average, eight late pick-ups per week per day care center.

In the fifth week, the fine was introduced. It was announced that any parent arriving more than 10 minutes late would pay $3 per child for each incident. The fee would be added to the parents' monthly bill, which was roughly $380.

After the fine was introduced, the number of late pick-ups promptly went not down, but up. Before long there were 20 late pick-ups per week, more than double the original average.

How could it be that financial incentives intended to diminish the number of late pick-ups actually increased them? Why did the incentives backfire?

As in the 1990s, when CEOs' stock options were blamed for creating negative incentives that led to many of the falsified earning reports at firms such as Enron and Worldcom, in the wake of the 2008 crisis, bankers' incentives have received significant public scrutiny, as many believe that they contributed to the crisis. This belief has led several governments and banking regulators around the world to introduce regulations on bankers' compensation.

Incentives are important in steering behavior and adaptation. Ill-designed incentive schemes that focus people and organizations on short-term objectives can create disincentives to investing in the future and adapting for the long term.

Incentives, therefore, deserve a chapter in this book as the fourth factor of organizational rigidity. To underscore the importance of incentives: in *Freakonomics* (which contains the aforementioned story of the day care centers on pages 15 and 16), University of Chicago economist Steven Levitt and *New York Times* journalist Stephen Dubner argue that economics is, in essence, the study of incentives (Levitt and Dubner 2005).

The Limits of Monetary Incentives

Monetary incentives are the bedrock of today's employee motivation and change management programs. The logic is simple and straightforward: change the monetary incentives and the desired behavior will occur.

The theoretical basis for money as an effective motivator is well researched. Generally, several studies have shown that money is effective in attracting, motivating, and retaining employees, and creating a high performance culture (Stajkovic and Luthans 1997; Peterson and Luthans 2006).

Monetary incentives tend to be most effective when there is a clear and immediate causal link between an individual action and a desired outcome, and when the desired outcome is easily measurable. For example, monetary incentives are effective in encouraging improved sales activities, such as incentivizing insurance agents (individually or as teams) to sell insurance products, or in investment banks.

The traditional concept of monetary incentives—in essence the positive reinforcement of expected behavior—goes back to the work of Burrhus Frederic Skinner, an American psychologist, and the Edgar Pierce Professor of Psychology at Harvard University from 1958 until his retirement in 1974.

Skinner—who was probably the most influential psychologist of the twentieth century (Haggbloom 2002)—was the founder of *Radical Behaviorism,* which posits that reinforcement is critical in influencing human behavior.

While strong and pervasive, financial incentives have serious limitations.

First, they tend to draw attention to and focus on activities and outcomes that are remunerated, while other activities, important as they may be for an organization, may not receive much attention. For example, when monetary incentives promote the achievement of the year's budget, many firms observe short-term-oriented behavior at the expense of long-term investments.

Second, financial incentives can also reduce desired social behavior, such as cross-unit collaboration. In a study published in 2002, Ernst Fehr of the University of Zurich and Armin Falk of the University of Bonn showed that monetary incentives targeted at promoting moral behavior may achieve the opposite and, in fact, undermine moral behavior.

They cite an experiment with Israeli high school students performed by two researchers, Uri Gneezy, holder of the Arthur Brody chair in behavioral economics at the Rady School of Management of the University of California in San Diego, and Aldo Rustichini, an economist at Cambridge University. Every year, on a predetermined day, students go from house to house collecting monetary donations from households for societies for cancer research, help for disabled children, and the like. Students performing these activities typically receive a great deal of social approval from parents, teachers, and other people. This is the very reason why they perform these activities voluntarily (Gneezy and Rustichini 2000). When students were each offered 1 percent of the money they collected, the amount collected decreased by 36 percent (Fehr and Falk 2002).

The short story at the beginning of the chapter, taken from Levitt's and Dubner's *Freakonomics* (but which also goes back to an experiment by Gneezy and Rustichini) is a further example. The day care center's fine of $3 replaced moral incentives (feelings of guilt on the part of the late-arriving parents) with monetary ones. For just a few dollars, parents could feel better and pay off their guilt. In addition, the small amount sent a signal to the parents saying that arriving late was no big deal, so why bother to be on time?

Third, monetary incentives used inappropriately can change the expectations of what people consider moral behavior. When monetary incentives replace moral incentives, this can lead to people changing the standards of what they perceive to be right or wrong. When, for example, the economists studying the day care centers eliminated the $3 fine in week seven, the number of late-arriving parents did not change. Parents no longer felt guilty about being late. Their moral sense had changed. So, it would seem that monetary incentives can change moral standards.

Fourth, excessive monetary rewards can lead to people cheating, especially if controls are lax and the chances of being caught are small (Levitt and Dubner 2005).

Recent findings in psychology suggest that monetary incentives should be used with caution and complemented by nonmonetary ones.

Effective (and Inexpensive) Nonmonetary Incentives

Psychology has developed a substantial body of knowledge in recent years about the functioning and power of nonfinancial incentives—social recognition, performance feedback, and working on intrinsically attractive tasks (Peterson and Luthans 2006; Fehr and Falk 2002). Nonmonetary incentives are believed to be at least as powerful as monetary incentives, even in situations in which monetary incentives work well. Furthermore, they seem to function well where monetary incentives typically fail.

Suzanne Peterson of Miami University and Fred Luthans of the University of Nebraska in Lincoln compared the relative impact of monetary and nonmonetary incentives on employees of a fast food chain in the United States. The conditions of their experiment were ideal for monetary incentives—there was a causal relation between action and outcome, and the outcome was measurable.

As an alternative to monetary incentives, they introduced two forms of nonfinancial incentive in selected fast food outlets: social recognition and performance feedback. Social recognition refers to the more informal acknowledgment, attention, praise, approval, or genuine appreciation for work well done by one individual or group. Performance feedback is defined as providing quantitative or qualitative information on past performance for the purpose of changing or maintaining that performance in specific ways. It conveys more task-relevant information to employees (Peterson and Luthans 2006).

The results of Peterson and Luthans' study indicated that both financial and nonfinancial incentives increased an outlet's performance significantly in regard to business unit profit, customer service, and employee turnover rates.

Interestingly, and even though the conditions for monetary incentives were ideal, nonmonetary incentives proved to be at least as powerful. Specifically, average profits rose 30 percent from preintervention to

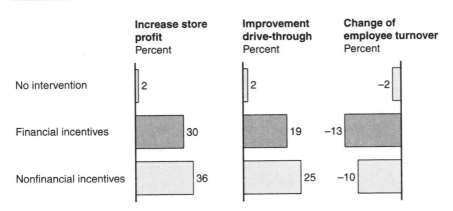

FIGURE 9.1   Effect of Monetary and Nonmonetary Incentives

Data source: Peterson, S. J., and F. Luthans. "The Impact of Financial and Nonfinancial Incentives on Business-Unit Outcomes over Time." *Journal of Applied Psychology* 91 (2006): 156–165.

postintervention (nine months) with monetary incentives, and 36 percent with nonmonetary incentives; drive-through times decreased 19 percent with monetary incentives, and 25 percent with nonmonetary ones; employee turnover improved 13 percent with monetary incentives, and 10 percent with nonmonetary ones (Peterson and Luthans 2006) (Figure 9.1).

These findings are consistent with those of Fehr and Falk. They demonstrate that nonmonetary incentives are powerful in shaping human behavior. Fehr and Falk analyzed three of them: the desire to reciprocate, the desire for social approval, and the desire to work on interesting tasks. The first two desires are social in nature. Many researchers believe that they are a product of our evolution, and are present in all humans regardless of race and origin. The third motive appears to originate in humans' (the brain's, actually) innate desire to learn and to progress (Fehr and Falk 2002).

Building Effective Incentive Systems

By and large, money seems to be a hygiene factor, important for recruiting and retention, and important for creating a performance culture. As noted, monetary incentives tend to be most appropriate when they lead to measurable, direct results that have an impact on the bottom line (profit and loss statement) or key performance indicators (KPI) clearly linked to the desired and incentivized behavior.

Money also works well when there is little room for cheating, that is, when there are no excessive rewards and when controls are rigorous. As mentioned earlier, monetary incentives typically work well with sales jobs.

However, money is not a great motivator. When basic factors such as fair and sufficient pay are in place, the additional performance boost from financial incentives is minimal, and nonmonetary incentives then become better motivators. These may include achievement, meaning, recognition, the intrinsic nature of the work itself, autonomy, opportunity for growth and advancement. As an example, 3M and Google provide free time to their employees so that they can spend work hours on special pet projects they are passionate about pursuing.

Ideally, therefore, a system will combine monetary and nonmonetary incentives. While highly effective, the use of nonmonetary incentives is more demanding—in two ways—for those, the leaders, who have to administer them.

First, the application of social recognition and performance feedback requires leadership skills. Social recognition, and performance feedback are most effective when (Peterson and Luthans 2006):

- Conveyed in a positive manner
- Delivered immediately after observing performance levels
- Represented visually, such as in graph or chart form
- Specific to the behavior that is being targeted for feedback
- Leaders consequently need to be trained to administer nonmonetary incentives effectively

Second, the use of nonmonetary incentives requires a high level of integrity and ethical behavior from leaders. The administration of non-monetary incentives is effective only when the administering leader visibly performs the expected social behavior. In other words, role modeling is essential (Dineen, Lewicki, and Tomlinson 2006).

More generally, and for both monetary as well as nonmonetary incentives, an effective incentive system needs to meet six criteria. First, people know their roles and understand exactly what is expected of them. Second, people have the capabilities, authority, information, and resources required to deliver on the results expected. Third, people know exactly what *good* looks like, so the key factor in unleashing higher performance is motivation and the will to demonstrate the required behaviors. Fourth, bonuses are appropriately tied to good behavior and good outcomes. Fifth, the orga-nization uses a fair and accurate system to measure outcomes and assess performance (while controlling compliance with regulations and policies).

Sixth and last, people get frequent and constructive feedback on whether and how past performance deviates from desired standards.

■ ■ ■

The situation created by AHD's financial incentives, which were designed to foster collaboration, was becoming more grotesque and less collaborative by the day.

Some people were paying not to go to meetings, so as to use the time to develop warm leads instead. At $1,000 per lead, creating warm leads could be quite a profitable activity, and the best thing about it was that it could be done during office hours.

Others were demanding to be rewarded for attending coordination meetings within the divisions. They argued that these meetings were also a form of collaboration.

One day, an alarmed auditor alerted a divisional head about a problem in his unit's incentive program tallies. The divisional head alerted Monica, who confirmed the serious problem the auditor had spotted. They caught an AHD employee cheating on a large scale. He had received more than $30,000 in rewards for creating a large number of warm leads. At first nobody noticed that, while the names of the medical practices he provided differed each time, they all had the same address and telephone number. Most sales to long-standing customers were made in person: A sales representative would visit the doctor's office and present the products. Not, however, sales to new, potential customers. They would be sold mostly over the phone; that is, salespeople would call potential customers and then visit only if the call indicated the possibility of a significant volume of sales.

The fraud was real, but the backstory might have been apocryphal. The tale being told in AHD's corridors was that, apparently, the employees' grandmother was at the other end of the telephone line. She had been a gifted actress in her youth, and she loved to engage salespeople in endless discussions. She never placed an order in the end, but that didn't matter, for the reward was due on the provision of the lead, not the closure of the deal. Making the sale was the responsibility of the sales representative, not of whoever provided the lead.

Amusing as it may sound (and even though it wasn't really clear whether it was actually true), the story of the employee and his grandmother created an uproar among the board members, who instantly scrapped all incentives to foster collaboration; overnight, an entire catalogue of rewards and fines was trash.

But how then to get people to collaborate? In their pivotal conversation, Felix had told Carl about nonmonetary incentives and had explained that people are intrinsically altruistic and motivated to collaborate.

Carl decided to try to build on nonmonetary incentives to foster collaboration. This was obviously a matter of leadership skills, and these skills were in short supply in AHD Group. Carl knew he had to reach deeply into his organization in some other way. With the support of the GET, he embarked on a project with one of the world's leading business schools to develop a *leadership development* program for AHD Group's top 1,000 leaders.

The program, a combination of classes and on-the-job training, took almost six months to set up, and it was costly. But the setup succeeded. Carl's new program could train a batch of roughly 200 leaders each month, with the attention of the appropriate GET members and their staffers.

The results were very encouraging, and after six months, the organization started to feel different. Overall, working for the AHD Group became more enjoyable, as an increasing number of executives and managers went through the training program. People generally felt more self-confident as their leadership and collaborative skills grew, and cross-unit collaboration was clearly stronger than ever before.

One day, Jerry—a rock-solid senior sales manager who had joined AHD in its early years—approached Carl, who knew him well from various senior management meetings, and took him aside in the hallway. Jerry, who was generally considered an *eminence grise* in the organization, grinned warmly. "I've been wanting to talk to you privately for a while, Carl," he said, "I'm glad I ran into you. I want you to know that I see the way you are changing the culture and spirit of this organization."

Carl looked at him, a little taken aback, as Jerry put his slightly battered briefcase down on the floor, crossed his arms and explained, "We have always been good at selling products. In fact, we've always been the best in our industry, and maybe beyond. Our sales culture is absolutely unbeatable, and we're all proud of it. We always make our numbers. But we've also always had problems collaborating. AHD always felt like a pool full of sharks."

Carl had to nod in understanding as Jerry continued, "Carl, you're starting to change this. While we are still the best sales guys out there, AHD is becoming a great place to work, and it is fun working together with colleagues to develop new solutions and new ideas. It's a great change...." He grinned again, picked up his briefcase and started to head down the hall, saying as he left, "Keep going, Carl!"

Carl stood still, savoring Jerry's words. This was quite a moment! Never in all these years had he felt so proud.

By now, AHD was doing really well. As the recession deepened, sales at AHD accelerated. The organization was now growing at more than 20 percent per annum, net of any acquisitions. It was leading the industry on growth, and profitability was very strong. Its profit margins were very high and clearly above those of its main competitors.

And all this had happened during a 24-month recession. AHD Group's stock price soared, while most competitors lost value and several went bankrupt. With AHD Group's stock becoming a very strong currency, now was the time to look for acquisitions.

CHAPTER 10

Fast Learners

In 1980, before Johnson & Johnson entered the consumer optical products business, its executives engaged in a strategic review and selected contact lenses as a promising new proposition, given the growth prospects, the lack of entrenched players, and the potential fit with the company's distribution strength and consumer reputation.

To turn the idea into practice, Johnson & Johnson took an exploratory first step. In 1981, it acquired Frontier Contact Lenses, a small $50 million company with a market share of less than 5 percent in the hard contact lens business. Frontier produced lenses using a traditional two-step molding and grinding process. This small acquisition gave Johnson & Johnson a starting point from which to learn the contact lens business.

Soon after the purchase, a manager from another Johnson & Johnson business encountered a Danish scientist who had developed a process for molding soft contact lenses. He realized that it might revolutionize the industry and called the president of Vistakon, Johnson & Johnson's contact lens business, who flew to Denmark the next day. The company snapped up the rights to a new polymer that could in theory be molded to the specification of a contact lens and cured via ultraviolet light. Produced in a new one-step process, it had the potential to slash production costs.

Vistakon realized that affordable disposable lenses could be marketed to consumers frustrated with the care hard lenses demanded. Johnson & Johnson still had to work out how to overcome the limitations of injection-molding technology to produce disposable contact lenses. Vistakon sought the assistance of NYPRO, one of the few companies capable of producing injection-molded lenses to the specifications required for human use.

Three years after its initial move, Johnson & Johnson had learned a great deal about the industry. It had also acquired a distinctive technology and manufacturing skills that made the venture less vulnerable to competitive attack. Its moves had been relatively small up to that point, but in the next few years, it committed some $250 million to bring the Surevue contact lens to market, and an additional $200 million to develop and launch the Acuvue disposable daily lens. By the mid-1990s, it had built a highly profitable business. By the 2000s it was the world's largest player in contact lenses.

The creation of Johnson & Johnson's contact lenses business is an excellent example of capturing wealth creation opportunities by exploiting existing capabilities (for example, distribution strength and consumer reputation) and by developing new ones over time. The case described above was researched and written up by Mehrdad Baghai, Stephen Coley, and David White, three colleagues at McKinsey, and authors of *The Alchemy of Growth* (Baghai, Coley, and White 1999).

However, counterintuitively, capabilities can also limit growth and adaptation, and can represent an important organizational rigidity, the fifth and last one we will analyze.

Defining Capabilities

Baghai, Coley, and White believe that a firm's capabilities provide the platform for it to grow, to develop competitive advantage, and to capture opportunities to create wealth. Broadly defined, capabilities encompass all the resources that a firm possesses. Baghai, Coley, and White categorize capabilities into four types: operational skills, privileged assets, growth-enabling capabilities, and special relationships.

First, *operational skills*. Operational skills are capabilities embedded in a company's people, processes, and institutional knowledge. These are often referred to as core competencies. They may include manufacturing skills, marketing skills, R&D skills, or product design know-how (Baghai, Coley, and White 1999).

Second, *privileged assets*. Privileged assets are physical or intangible assets that are hard to replicate and provide competitive advantage to their owner. They include distribution networks, brands and reputation, customer information, and intellectual property (Baghai, Coley, and White 1999).

Third, *growth-enabling skills*. Some organizations have generic growth-enabling skills such as acquisition, deal structuring, finance, risk management, and capital management. While operational skills and privileged assets tend to be specific to each of a company's businesses, these growth-enabling skills are more generic and transferable from one market or business unit to another. Because of their broad applicability, they are usually developed in the corporate center, which makes them available to all of the business units (Baghai, Coley, and White 1999).

Fourth, *special relationships*. Relationships can be an important capability. For example, relationships with existing customers can provide growth opportunities through cross-selling. Those with powerful individuals, businesses, and governments can create opportunities that would otherwise not exist. In particular, relationships may enable entry into new industries and geographies, and make deals possible (Baghai, Coley, and White 1999).

Capabilities as a Constraint to Adaptation

The concept of developing a firm by building on existing resources, and by developing new ones, is not new. It goes back to Edith Penrose, a British economist, who during her career taught at Johns Hopkins University, at the London School of Economics, and at INSEAD in France.

While at Johns Hopkins, Penrose participated in a research project on the growth of firms. She came to the conclusion that existing theories were not sufficient to explain how firms grow and develop (Beinhocker 2006).

In 1959, she published her book *The Theory of the Growth of the Firm*. In theorizing about companies that grow, Dr. Penrose wrote: "There are important administrative restraints on the speed of the firm's growth. Human resources required for the management of change are tied to the individual firm and so are internally scarce. Expansion requires the recruitment of more such resources. New recruits cannot become fully effective overnight. The growth process is, therefore, dynamically constrained" (Penrose 1959).

Penrose linked the ability of firms to grow to the available resources and to the need to develop these resources over time.

A firm is restricted in the wealth-creation opportunities it can capture. Its existing assets and resources determine those opportunities. A car manufacturer, for example, is unlikely to have the capabilities and resources to create a contact lens business. However, as companies implement their strategies, they may develop new resources and capabilities that can open up new areas of opportunity for wealth creation.

Beinhocker describes this relationship between strategy implementation and capability development as "the co-evolution of resources and business plans." It creates a path to dependence in how organizations can adapt and react to changes in the environment (Beinhocker 2006). As an example, a firm will probably not develop from being a tire manufacturer into being a high-tech PC manufacturer overnight.

Building Capabilities Fast

Companies rarely possess all the capabilities they need to succeed in new businesses and new environments. But, strategically, they can choose between four approaches for fast-forwarding the development of capabilities.

First, firms can fast-build capabilities. As we have seen in Chapters 4 and 5, engaging the front line in solving problems, having self-confident people in pivotal roles, and embedding changes in organizational processes can fast-forward the building of new capabilities.

Second, firms can borrow capabilities. They can borrow them from other organizations by embarking on alliances, partnerships, or licensing agreements.

Third, firms can buy capabilities. They can buy them by hiring new people, procuring additional technologies, or acquiring entire companies.

Four, firms can keep spare capabilities in stock. By making venture investments and by pursuing several smaller strategic moves in areas of potential interest, firms can hold a large number of capabilities, larger than those needed for the implementation of its current strategy.

Holding in stock means experimenting. It may mean running different strategies, even competing ones, in parallel. Microsoft's strategy in the late 1980s is one of the best examples of this tactic, since it simultaneously pursued six quite different strategies to gain the leadership of the market for operating systems (Beinhocker 2006).

Another example is HSBC's geographic expansion strategy in the 1980s. Instead of focusing on a few countries, HSBC entered a large number of emerging markets in parallel and much earlier than its competitors. HSBC did not know which markets would eventually grow and develop into attractive banking markets. But being in many more markets than its competitors increased the likelihood of HSBC having a position in the right market at the right time.

However, people do not like experimenting in an organizational context. By definition, experiments can fail, and most organizations do not reward failure. To foster experimentation, leaders may need to base their assessments on criteria other than outcomes. They may want to ask questions such as: "How committed are people to experimentation? How many small experiments have they run, and how well have they extracted lessons from their efforts, their risk assessments, and the mistakes they have made?"

Organizations that do not reward smart experimentation and smart risk-taking, even when the outcome is unsatisfactory, may risk losing valuable, courageous, innovative, and creative people to other organizations. They may lose the very capabilities most needed for adaptation (Heifetz, Grashow, and Linsky 2009).

■ ■ ■

The value of most firms in the industry was deflated, but since AHD's stock was a great currency, Carl decided to take advantage of the situation.

The future of the industry was far from clear. Many analysts and industry observers forecast doom and gloom. They predicted the rise of additional large hospital purchasing organizations that would put pressure on profit margins. They wrote extensively about expected regulatory changes that would seriously limit the reimbursement of products and services provided by AHD Group. Competition from the Far East, especially in the implants businesses, was also a concern.

Many new technologies were emerging in diagnostics and implants that were about three to four years from market launch, though it was unclear which ones would make it to the market, if any. Despite this lack of certainty, some of the technologies were of great interest to AHD Group.

AHD Group had rebuilt its reputation for great products and service quality in the industry; it had three strong product lines protected by several patents; it had truly exceptional sales and innovation capabilities; and it possessed special relationships with exclusive partners delivering high quality products to complement its own offering. And thanks to the leadership development program, client outreach, patient visits, and the rest of the initiatives Carl and his team had launched, AHD's internal organization was functioning more smoothly than ever before in its history. A strong position, Carl thought.

Toward the end of the recession, when it looked as if stock prices in the industry had started rising again, AHD made five acquisitions within six months. This was a firework display for AHD Group, which hadn't made any acquisitions in the five years since Carl had taken over as CEO.

Four of the acquisitions were very small, and the markets and analysts hardly noticed them. Three were minor investments in market segments adjacent to orthopedics and dental, and one was in a new digital imaging technology. Carl regarded them as small experiments. They might eventually make a return, but maybe not.

One acquisition, though, was much larger. This was the acquisition of ImagingCo, a company producing and marketing X-ray machines. There was a clear rationale. The company was—in Carl's and the board's view—undervalued because it had lost its innovative edge in recent years.

ImagingCo had been the innovation leader in its niche, but lack of cash to fund experiments or even to underwrite small investments in more recent technologies, as well as the loss of a few talented researchers, had damaged its ability to continue a stream of innovative product launches. Furthermore, ImagingCo had never had outstanding sales and distribution capabilities. Carl and the GET felt that it had huge potential. With the open architecture concept, AHD could reignite the flame of innovation at ImagingCo, and with the help of AHD's sales force, the company could regain its edge in the market.

Market analysts applauded the acquisition. ImagingCo's and AHD Group's stock prices rose 27 percent and 4 percent, respectively, on the announcement of the acquisition. The reputation and credibility that the AHD Group and its management enjoyed with the equity markets was very, very strong.

AHD Group was now well diversified and prepared for the future. It had four substantial business units (Dental Inc and ImagingCo were separate legal entities), with leadership positions and a high level of profitability in four large and growing market segments: imaging, orthopedic implants, dental implants, and diagnostics.

It had created two new firms, GBS and AHDM, which now had started to successfully provide services to third parties beyond the AHD Group. Also, the Group possessed a series of smaller assets that at the time had an almost experimental character, but which might be big businesses one day. And it had potent skills in research and development and sales and distribution.

The organization felt confident and proud of itself. The enthusiasm and energy in the group was pervasive. Even visitors could feel it.

By now, Carl knew that he had made the right choice in continuing to lead AHD. He had his legacy: the AHD Group itself.

PART **IV**

Serial Innovators

CHAPTER 11

The Secrets of Serial Innovators

Organizations age and die. They do so because—as they grow and mature—they develop rigidities, at both individual and organizational levels. The process of aging seemingly unfolds slowly, inexorably, and naturally—similar to the processes of aging in biological organisms.

It seems to unfold naturally, but it doesn't. The aging of organizations is not a natural, or biological, process. Rigidities—both individual and organizational—are man-made. They originate in two areas: in the human brain, and in organizational constructs composed of human beings.

First, our reviews have shown that the *human brain* regularly develops rigidities in the form of biases, lack of self-confidence, and habits. As we have seen earlier, the human brain is limited in what it can process. It works with shortcuts or rules of thumb to solve problems it faces regularly. The human brain embodies successful (and unsuccessful) rules of thumb, and over time these become mental models (or simply experience); they become the way to think about a problem or an issue. These mental models are highly efficient. They allow quick decision making and action, especially when confronted with familiar challenges, and when there is a need to act under time pressure. They can represent a major risk, however, when the context in which they were developed, or the marketplace, changes significantly. As we have seen earlier, they may make people unable to correctly diagnose a problem or to apply the appropriate problem-solving approach.

The following statement, made in 1977 by Ken Olson, the founder of Digital Equipment Corporation, is an example of mental models at work: "There is no reason why anyone would want a computer in their home."

Also, in our story of Carl, the refusal of the board and of the GET to even accept the notion that AHD was struggling, the inability to diagnose the challenges that the organization was facing, the inability to change behavior, even when the need for change was recognized, are powerful examples of mental models at work.

Second, *organizations* regularly develop rigidities. Structures, performance management and reward systems, supporting cultures, capabilities (or simply collective experience) are human constructs that allow firms— groups of individuals—to fulfill their common mission and to implement strategies at scale effectively and efficiently. Without them, performing large tasks or implementing complex strategies requiring the effective and efficient collaboration of hundreds or thousands of individuals would not be possible. However, as with mental models, these constructs—organizational charts and reporting lines, performance management and reward systems, the organizational culture, capabilities or institutional experience—are rigidities that may prevent organizations from adapting rapidly when markets change. Also, organizational rigidities tend to grow over time. To deal with the increasing complexity and demands of dynamic markets, and to capture ever more wealth-creation opportunities, firms tend to add additional functions, councils, processes, values, and norms onto existing organizations. Only seldom do firms eliminate older organizational constructs that have become obsolete—older processes, older functions, or older committees. As a consequence, layers of new constructs are added onto older ones, making firms bureaucratic, inward-oriented, and slow in adapting to changes in the market.

The increasing organizational complexity of AHD, as its management added function after function, layer after layer, to help them cope with increasing market demands and a complex strategy, may serve as an example of creeping rigidities in practice. It is an illustration of how—with the best of intentions by the management team, and with a drive to capture ever more value—organizational rigidities nevertheless develop and grow.

While the connotation may imply something negative, rigidities per se are neither good nor bad. They are simply necessary for human beings and organizations to function effectively and efficiently. However—sometimes, and in particular in times of change—they can become the reason for organizational failure, decay, and firm death.

So the question isn't how can we prevent rigidities from developing, but rather how can we contain them and how can we complement them to maintain organizational adaptability and to cultivate innovation?

Our reviews of the various academic fields have shown that informed and thoughtful interventions can interrupt or at least slow down the process of the aging of firms.

Seven interventions seem particularly relevant:

1. Cultivating the firm's members' desire to make a difference.
2. Building a team of learners at the top.

3. Framing the vision and strategy positively.
4. Building on self-managed performance cells.
5. Promoting the firm's members' drive to perform and grow.
6. Investing in capabilities to quickly develop new assets and skills.
7. Cultivating a culture that fosters execution and promotes challenge.

Let's explore the seven interventions one by one.

Cultivating the Desire to Make a Difference

It's not because of the amount of money. For me and my colleagues, the most important thing is that we create an open information flow for people.

—Mark Zuckerberg, founder, Facebook

The first intervention is to leverage the desire of human beings to contribute to something that matters and to make a difference in life. It is to define the purpose of the firm as being to make a difference to people, by developing new products and services that make the life of their customers safer, healthier, richer, better, more valuable. The firm would satisfy the requirements of its stakeholders, also of its shareholders, as boundary conditions for its strategy, but it would not be driven by the desire to generate more profit or to maximize shareholder value.

Traditional economics argues that the purpose of a business is to maximize shareholder value. It believes that the business that seeks to generate profit and maximize shareholder value is instrumental in helping society to allocate resources optimally and in creating efficient markets. This belief is so deeply rooted that several countries, including the United States and the United Kingdom, have spelled out the legal obligations and fiduciary duties of boards and managements of public companies to act in the best interest of their shareholders (Beinhocker 2006).

Over the past decades, well before the last financial crisis, several academics and researchers raised concerns about putting shareholders' interests above those of other stakeholders. They put forward alternative views that call for a more balanced approach of creating value for the various stakeholder groups of the corporation: shareholders, customers, employees, governments and regulators, and society as a whole. They argue that only such an approach can create the conditions for sustainable, long-term shareholder value creation.

Traditional economists disagree. They argue that systems focused on creating value for multiple stakeholders lack clarity, create confusion by trying to balance competing interests, and serve society less well than the shareholder value–based approach. They also argue that *in theory* maximizing shareholder value requires taking a sustainable and value-creating approach to multiple stakeholders anyway, so what's the point of changing the target function?

The problem lies not in theory but *in practice;* specifically in the way management attempts to achieve the objective of maximizing shareholder value. More often than not, companies articulate the shareholder value objective through a focus on stock price movements and quarterly results. A survey of more than 400 chief financial officers by the U.S. Federal Bureau of Economic Research concluded that the majority of the companies surveyed consider quarterly earnings as the key metric for maximizing shareholder value. In the same survey, a majority of the chief financial officers mentioned that they would forgo value-creating long-term investments if it meant missing their earnings targets (Beinhocker 2006).

Eric Beinhocker, a young economist, believes that shareholder value should not be an objective in and of itself; rather, it should be seen as a fundamental constraint, as a boundary condition, that has to be met for business to succeed. His view is echoed by many academics who have studied the concept of company longevity. Collins and Porras, the authors of *Built to Last,* summarized the point as follows: "Profit is like oxygen, food, water, and blood for the body; they are not the point of life, but without them there is no life" (Collins and Porras 1994).

But if not shareholder value, what should drive a company?

Beinhocker takes an evolutionary perspective on this question and puts forward the thesis that the ultimate objective of a company should be to survive and to replicate, or grow (Beinhocker 2006). He argues that firms surviving for longer periods of time, while satisfying the boundary conditions of creating value for the various stakeholders, including shareholders, end up creating more net present value for their shareholders than short-lived investors' favorites.

However, companies are not biological cells whose sole purpose is to survive and replicate (or grow). Organizations consist of human beings. The brains of human beings are predisposed to a search for meaning. People naturally (neuronally, in fact) long to make a difference in their lives. People spend a significant part of their lives at work, so that firms and employees can both profit when they act passionately in the same cause.

Thus, the purpose would be to make a difference, while delivering an adequate return to its stakeholders. A difference to what? Insights from psychology and anthropology gained in Carl's journey would suggest that people have an *altruistic bias*, an innate need to help and support others, especially if these others are less healthy, as is the case with patients, or less fortunate in life. It seems that companies that focus on helping others are powerful in providing meaning to their members. These are not companies with mission statements like "Our mission is to be the company most admired for its people and performance" or "Our mission is to grow profitably," but those with mission statements such as "Our mission is to improve patients' lives" or "To promote the financial well-being of our customers and their families."

A phrase by Steve Jobs, Apple's chairman and former CEO, illustrates the point. In 1983, Jobs approached John Sculley, an executive at Pepsi-Cola, asking him to join his team and to serve as Apple's CEO. "Do you want to sell sugar water for the rest of your life, or do you want to come with me and change the world?" Jobs asked Sculley. The question shows that for Jobs, Apple is a way to make a difference in life.

Leveraging people's passion to make a difference can backfire, however, and quickly result in widespread cynicism if it is done in a manipulative manner. A firm's purpose should therefore be first and foremost *honest* and meaningful (meaning-full) to the firm's leaders, and they should *visibly commit* to it, well beyond mere words. Visibly committing means investing leadership time, incurring costs, or forgoing other gains.

Also, leaders may want to build on their own experiences and emotions. Then a firm purpose needs to be brought to life with *inspiring stories and metaphors, and by using emotions.* As we have seen earlier, our brain organizes our thinking as stories. It can handle narratives much better than lists or facts. Also, it is better at memorizing stories that appeal to emotions (and are told frequently).

Building a Team of Learners at the Top

> *My model for business is the Beatles: They were four guys that kept each other's negative tendencies in check; they balanced each other. And the total was greater than the sum of the parts. Great things in business are not done by one person; they are done by a team of people.*
> —Steve Jobs, chairman and former chief executive officer, Apple

It is essential to have teams made up of people with diverse mental models, people with a strong belief in their own self-efficacy, and people whose purpose is aligned with that of the firm, staffed in positions that are important for the company in adapting to changes in its environment. Some organizational areas or departments—such as research and development, marketing, or technology—may be more important for adaptation than others.

The top leadership team, the executive management, is certainly a key area for company adaptation. Getting the composition and the dynamics of the top team right is likely to be the central to company adaptation and innovation.

The members of a top team in the new model organization are likely to need four characteristics.

First, they will need to have a *strong sense of self-efficacy*. Leaders with this inner strength set higher goals, apply better problem-solving techniques, and are more resilient.

Second, members of the top team will need to have a *positive attitude towards learning*. Individuals with this mindset are more flexible and adaptive. They are less defensive of their own past work and tend to view challenges and setbacks not as personal failures but as learning experiences.

Third, top-team members will need to have *diverse mental models*. Peoples' mental models are shaped by their experiences, as people come to see things differently when their experiences vary. Diversity of mental models, especially at the top, is a huge asset for companies in dynamic and complex environments. If they have a broad set of experiences and mental models, leaders are more likely to recognize new, unfamiliar challenges when they arise.

Fourth, they will need to be able to *work in teams*. Self-efficacy, a learning attitude, and diversity are not sufficient if people do not collaborate, and work in teams. Members of a well-performing team must be aligned on goals, encourage critical challenges through effective dialogues, and regularly assess themselves as a unit (Frisch 2008; Herb, Leslie, and Price 2001). This may seem obvious; however, in a recent article in the *Harvard Business Review,* Richard Rosen and Fred Adair, from the executive search firm Heidrick & Struggles, reported that according to a survey of 60 top HR executives from Fortune 500 companies, only 6 percent of the executives would describe the top leadership of their companies as a well-integrated team (Rosen and Adair 2007).

As Scott Keller, Michiel Kruyt, and Judy Malan of McKinsey's Organization Practice put it: "Having a high-performing top team helps companies to innovate, to pursue cross-cutting business opportunities, and to stay open and adaptable to change as new challenges arise" (Keller, Kruyt, and Malan 2010).

However, the CEO does not always have a perfect team, and his freedom to make changes may be limited by a lack of alternatives, by fear of the loss of specific knowledge, or by the fact that he has previously made commitments to specific people.

It may be important to assess members of the top team not only on their existing characteristics, but also on their ability to develop the necessary characteristics that they lack. We have seen earlier (neuroplasticity) that—when prompted—people can be capable of significant changes in attitude and capabilities.

Positively Framing the Vision and Strategy

Leaders need to be optimists. Their vision is beyond the present.
—Rudy Giuliani, former mayor of New York City

Members of an organization are more likely to engage in problem-solving and behavioral change that happens in a positively loaded emotional context. A *positively framed direction*—engaging visions of the future and convincing strategies to get there—appealing to positive emotions (that keep the amygdalae relaxed), helps nudge people into continuous problem-solving and learning, and makes firms adaptive.

Steve Jobs's turnaround at Apple shows the impact of positive framing, of providing a direction that is simple, positive, and emotional. When he returned to the company after a long exile, he reframed the image of Apple from being a marginalized player fighting for few points of market share to being the home of a small but enviable elite: The creators who dared to "Think different" (Deutschman 2005).

This view is in stark contrast with the recommendations of many change gurus, who put forward the view that firms need to develop burning platforms in order to change continuously. The fundamental problem with this view is that it misses the way firms actually adapt, morph, and change continuously. While it is true that situations loaded with negative emotions lead to changes in behavior, firms are unlikely to be in extreme crisis situations, such as imminent bankruptcy, all the time. Continuously and artificially creating crises for the sake of continuous change may end up breeding cynicism and making change efforts void (Bandura 1997).

This does not mean that when a firm finds itself in a challenging environment, and when several trends are affecting it negatively, its leaders should talk only about positive developments. People are not naive, and in today's information-intense world, members of organizations often know all about the problems and challenges that their organization is facing. Denying challenges will only foster cynicism and may be as counterproductive as continuously creating artificial crises.

A firm's leadership should ideally acknowledge its challenges openly and engage the organization in fact-based, articulated, realistic, but positively framed movement forward.

Building on Self-Managed Performance Cells

The company was quite hierarchical. I often think it was like a pyramid. [. . .] I try to turn the pyramid upside down so that I'm at the bottom and bubbling away and encouraging people and energizing them so that they are all empowered so that they can do what they need to do. Now, that's the dream.
                                            —Janet Holmes à Court, Australian businesswoman

The fourth intervention is building on self-managed performance cells, autonomous organizational units that leverage the goal orientation, drive to succeed, and creativity of human beings.

One of the first applications of the concept of autonomous units was the reorganization of General Motors (GM) by Alfred Sloan, its long-standing president and chairman. In the 1950s, he reorganized GM into five divisions, effectively five independent car companies, each with its own brand and its own profit and loss statement. This allowed GM to grow and—at the time—to become the world's largest company (Beinhocker 2006).

This concept has since been applied in many companies and industries, as they have reorganized into business-unit structures. In the past decade—inspired by firms such as IBM and Procter & Gamble—several corporations have started to apply the concept of the notional company to other areas as well, creating manufacturing companies and so-called global business support (GBS) companies, specialized firms providing shared back-office services such as accounting, payroll services, and infrastructure services.

The concept doesn't stop at the level of business units or notional manufacturing and service companies, however. It can be applied much lower down the organizational hierarchy. Inspired by the kaizen concept at Toyota, many firms have created more autonomous, self-managed teams in a large variety of functions. We now often find them in functions such as sales, manufacturing, or back-office operations. These teams are often referred to as *lean teams*.

Self-managed performance cells have three characteristics.

First, they are guided by *performance metrics*. Depending on the specific objectives and activities of the team, these metrics can be very different. In sales or customer management, they would include cross-selling rates, revenues, or service quality. In production, they would include default rates, scrap rates, or unit costs. The challenge is to get the right set of performance metrics. Get too many or get the metrics wrong and you get unintended results. When selecting the relevant data for performance management, organizations need to make sure that the data set is not too large, but at the same time is well balanced (Kaplan and Norton 1992; Dobbs and Koller 2005). Sometimes organizations that suffer from poor adaptation are overloaded with data. Hence, learning is delayed as different people involved in the team look at different subsets of data and fail to agree on a diagnosis of the problem.

Second, they have the *ability to organize themselves* to continuously improve the outcome or results. This means that they are delegated the responsibility for decisions on the resources that are most pertinent for achieving their objectives (for example, hiring or making investments within decision limits). It should be noted that there is a significant amount of literature suggesting that autonomy or participative management should be limited and focused on the organization of the work of the cells (self-management), as opposed to cells setting their own targets (which we would call *self-directed teams*). Several studies suggest that teams that self-set their targets may record higher levels of employee satisfaction, but not of performance (Bandura 1997).

Third, they have *periodic sessions for learning* and joint problem solving ("finding and embedding new mental patterns"). Depending on the size and nature of the performance cell, these sessions may happen yearly (the planning and budgeting process of a division, for example), in quarterly or monthly performance reviews, or in weekly or daily team problem-solving sessions (in Toyota's kaizen, for example).

Promoting the Firm's Drive to Perform and Grow

Outstanding leaders go out of the way to boost the self-esteem of their personnel. If people believe in themselves, it's amazing what they can accomplish.

—Sam Walton, founder and former president, Wal-Mart

The fifth intervention is to go beyond pay for performance and monetary incentives to motivate employees. The fifth intervention wants to recognize the performance of the firm members, to build their self-confidence, to foster their passion to achieve ambitious goals, and to help them to grow their abilities.

The fifth intervention acts on two main levers: on the performance management and reward system, and on leadership development.

On *performance management and rewards.* The first lever is to set ambitious but achievable goals, to use individualized performance feedback, and to use both monetary and nonmonetary incentives to reward firm members.

Ambitious but achievable goals are engaging, and foster motivation and innovative thinking. As seen earlier, positive achievements support the development of self-efficacy. Achieving ambitious goals builds self-confidence, leads to better problem-solving, and gets people to set even higher goals for themselves.

Many firms have practices built into their performance appraisal systems that foster a low sense of efficacy. Some firms sort their employees into ability groups (so-called forced rankings), which convert performance evaluations into negative experiences for most, and which over time lead to a depletion of self-confident performers in an organization. On the contrary, firms may work with individualized performance assessments—in which the ratings are relative to individual achievements (deviation from budget or degree of individual target achievement, for example). Individualized assessments are more powerful in developing a large cadre of self-confident, adaptive, and resilient members of an organization.

Finally, firms may use both monetary and nonmonetary incentives to reward its members. Monetary incentives are effective in attracting, motivating, and retaining employees, and creating a high performance culture (Stajkovic and Luthans 1997, 2003). Monetary incentives tend to be most effective when there is a clear and immediate causal link between an individual action and a desired outcome, and when the desired outcome is easily measurable. For example, monetary incentives are effective in encouraging improved sales activities, such as incentivizing insurance agents to sell insurance products. However, monetary incentives also have drawbacks, and the new model complements them by making extensive use of nonmonetary incentives, including achievement, recognition, the intrinsic nature of the work itself, autonomy, opportunity for growth, and advancement.

On *leadership development.* Setting ambitious, but achievable goals, providing individualized feedback, managing nonmonetary rewards, but also leading autonomous performance cells—whether at the level of a team, a project group, a department, or a business unit—requires experience and leadership capabilities.

It is hard to delegate decision-making power to autonomous performance cells if their leaders do not have problem-solving capabilities, the ability to lead teams, the ability to build the self-confidence of their team members, and the ability to take decisions. These capabilities are developed in people who aspire to become leaders, as much as in people who already are in leadership positions.

Firms may use different approaches to develop these capabilities.

Some focus on *selection,* starting at the recruiting level. Procter & Gamble, for example, devotes a great deal of attention to recruiting the right people, sometimes reviewing more than 50 resumes for one position.

Some organizations focus on developing management capabilities through *formal training programs,* a classic example being officers' training in the U.S. army. Another example of a broader training program is Chevron's mandatory Capital Stewardship Capability program, launched in 2000 by Chevron's CEO, David O'Reilly, to increase leadership and decision-making competence across the board.

Other organizations focus on *on-the-job training,* and regard the development of leadership capabilities as a line manager's task. One approach to fostering line responsibility for leadership development is to establish a norm of preparing succession plans. Managers who have good succession plans, and who are eager to progress in their own careers, often look for their replacement among the people who work for them, and are therefore more likely to develop them as leaders (Heifetz, Grashow, and Linsky 2009).

Finally, and also given the importance of cultivating different mental frameworks in leaders, some firms focus on *rotating* future leaders between different geographies, functions, and roles.

Building Capabilities to Quickly Develop New Assets and Skills

An organization's ability to learn, and translate that learning into action rapidly, is the ultimate competitive advantage.
—Jack Welch, retired chief executive officer, General Electric

A firm is restricted in the wealth-creation opportunities it can capture. At any one time, its existing assets and skills determine its opportunities.

Assets and skills that are needed to succeed in the market may include market-specific know-how (such as customer insights, or knowledge of a specific geographic market), functional capabilities (such as marketing, sales management, manufacturing, R&D), and know-how about potential emerging opportunities (such as technologies or relevant adjacent industries).

Since markets are dynamic and the sources of competitive advantage change continuously, companies rarely possess all the assets and skills they need to succeed in new businesses and new environments, and they need to be able to develop such assets and skills fast.

Firms may use four approaches to fast-forwarding the development of assets and skills: It can *fast-build* assets and skills (for example, engaging the front line in problem solving, having self-confident people in pivotal roles, and embedding changes in organizational processes); it can *borrow* capabilities (with alliances, partnerships, or licensing agreements); it can *buy* capabilities (for example, hiring new people, procuring additional technologies, or acquiring entire companies); alternatively, it can *experiment* (by making, for example, venture investments, or by pursuing several smaller strategic moves in areas of potential interest).

Cultivating a Culture That Fosters Execution and Promotes Challenge

From the very beginning we told our people, "Question it. Challenge it." Remember, decades of conventional wisdom have sometimes led the airline industry into huge losses.
—H. Kelleher, founder and former president, Southwest Airlines

Organizational culture can be leveraged to complement the organization's formal structure, and in reducing the need for dense hierarchies and processes. Culture can help guide the daily activities of employees in the absence of written rules or policies (Mallak 2001). It thus enables greater decentralization, providing general guidance, but leaving the specific *how* up to the individual, allowing more space for adaptation at the front line.

In recent years, numerous studies have explored building learning cultures and adapting corporate cultures. It is often argued that organizations need to create an environment in which people can exchange perspectives, debate matters, learn, and progress. While this is right, it is incomplete. It should be kept in mind that organizations are created to perform tasks: to implement and execute strategies and business plans.

A corporate culture will therefore probably be more effective when it makes use of values and cultural norms that foster both execution and innovation, or execution and renewal (Beinhocker 2006; Daft 2007; Keller and Price 2011). Execution values and norms, that is, getting things done, include, among other elements, strategy execution and collaboration (Klein 2008). Innovation or renewal values and norms include, among others, flexibility, challenge, and openness. Innovation or renewal values and norms facilitate challenging the organization and its people by "bringing the market into the organization."

In situations that are unfamiliar and infrequent, individuals, and hence organizations, are often subject to an optimism bias. For example, when a market situation changes—as when a new technology launched by a new market entrant is endangering an incumbent player (a situation that does not occur very often in the life cycle of a firm)—the managers of the incumbent firm tend to underweight the risks. They tend to look at the situation too optimistically, and often delay necessary changes.

On the other hand, organizations that are open to new ideas, firms that regularly and systematically *bring outside views and data into the organization,* are likely to be less prone to this bias.

Firms may use different approaches to get outside perspectives into the organization. Some may use the board of directors or a strategic advisory board as a source of information. Others may use second opinions or critical challenges of plans and strategies by external industry experts. Another approach may be the way some private equity firms address the optimism bias by always taking a fresh look: After a partner has supervised a company for a few years, a different partner evaluates it anew (Lovallo and Sibony 2006).

Whatever the approach, in continuously and intensely seeking external information and critical challenge, the new model is more likely to innovate, to adapt, and to recognize and capture opportunities for value creation when they arise.

Sometimes, but only sometimes, firms resist the aging process. These are firms that are driven by the passion to make a difference to customers and society; firms that are led by learners with an ambitious and positive vision; firms that are organized and build on their members' desire to achieve results, and their eagerness to grow and develop; firms that are quick in developing new capabilities; firms that, while focusing thoroughly on execution and results, remain externally oriented and continuously challenge themselves.

Such firms adapt and thrive in dynamic markets; they are serial innovators; they continuously reinvent themselves; they change their industries. Sometimes—by continuously inventing new products and services that make life healthier, better, and safer—they change the world.

These firms create value for decades, sometimes longer, for their customers, their shareholders, and their employees.

■ ■ ■

When he took over AHD as CEO, Carl had found a firm in disarray.

AHD had once enjoyed a good reputation as a provider of high quality products. This reputation had, however, been seriously damaged by quality issues with some of its products. With no clear sense of mission at the top, morale among the employees was, unsurprisingly, low. People were disengaged, and not prepared to take initiatives. Indeed, the quality problems that AHD had experienced could, Carl had found, be traced to dissatisfaction and lack of commitment on the part of the employees.

Also, he found himself confronted, not with a team of colleagues working to a common purpose, but with a collection of individuals concerned with cultivating their own gardens. Some of the board members had even lost confidence in the future of the firm.

A once-profitable company, AHD had ceased making money, and was not growing. Its inability to invest meant that it was missing out on technological innovations. More disturbing than the firm's economic state, however, was what Carl found when he sat around the table with his board and his executive team. This was an organization that had lost its way, and did not have the resources to get itself back on track again.

First, and most urgently, Carl had worked to reshape the firm's strategy to respond to the realities in the market and to use AHD's own strengths. With the open architecture approach that Carl brought from KenkoInc and developed at AHD, it was able to serve even its most demanding customers in an effective and cost-efficient way. Also, AHD had expanded into a number of new product segments and emerging, fast-growing markets.

By year four of Carl's tenure, in early 2008, AHD had started to grow rapidly. During the recession in 2009 and 2010, when the market hardly grew at all, AHD was the industry's fastest-growing firm, with an annual growth rate of more than 20 percent.

At the end of 2010, sales in new product segments and geographies amounted to 40 percent of total sales. As AHD grew, its profit soared. AHD earned world-class profitability. After six years, the AHD Group's revenues had nearly doubled, and profits had tripled.

However, what Carl had achieved at AHD went far beyond implementing an effective strategy.

When advocating the new business model, he had been amazed at the way many of his colleagues could not seem to understand problems that were so obvious to him. At first, some of these issues had seemed intractable to Carl, and the conventional solutions unsatisfactory. How was it possible for his colleagues not to see the obvious?

The search for answers to such questions had taken Carl into areas that he never expected to enter. His study of behavioral economics, in particular, set him on the path toward the successful remaking of AHD. It led him to investigate aspects of neuroscience, human psychology, and even spirituality. Armed with the insights from his investigations, Carl had transformed AHD into a healthy, vital organization.

With a noble mission to innovate and develop medical devices that would help cure patients, and a strategy based on an open architecture framework and on technological and geographic expansion, AHD had created a positive, inspiring context.

AHD was no longer the losing incumbent, but the elite of the industry. People were proud of working for AHD.

Carl had devoted much of his attention to the composition of teams: the board, the senior management team, and the teams managing the most organizational units.

He had also given the organization a flatter structure and—while greatly strengthening the management information systems and tightening up the incentive systems—he had restructured the firm into units, effectively empowering the people of AHD.

He hardwired the changes in an HR system that promoted job rotation and diversity. And he lived and shaped the values that were now the fabric of AHD: experimenting and working together to achieve results.

To foster experimentation, AHD had made small bets on new technologies. Analysts noted that AHD now had one of the industry's most valuable pipelines, guaranteeing its success for decades to come.

One of Carl's innovations had been to launch a Values Day, a one-day event that took place at every AHD subsidiary around the world on a specific day. On Values Day, employees discussed and debated the company's mission, values, and strategy. Participation was mandatory for everyone, executives, office clerks, workers, secretaries, receptionists, and drivers like Luke. Quite simply, it was mandatory for everyone. Carl led Values Day at the head office in person, while the country CEOs of the various divisions did so at their subsidiaries.

Under Carl's leadership, AHD had become a very different kind of organization.

CHAPTER 12

Beyond Business: The Medici, Oxford, and the Catholic Church

In the last chapter we summarized the findings of our journey by describing seven interventions to build a firm that adapts and thrives in dynamic markets; that is a serial innovator; that continuously reinvents itself; that changes its industry. Sometimes—by continuously inventing new products and services that make life healthier, better, safer—it changes the world.

Such a firm is driven by the desire to make a difference, is led by a team of learners, is framed positively, is built on self-managed performance cells that promote its members' drive to perform and grow, is quick to develop new assets and skills, and has a culture that fosters execution while simultaneously promoting challenge.

Can these interventions be helpful beyond the business context? Can we apply these interventions to other forms of institutions, to other forms of organizations composed of human beings, not only to the business corporation? Can we apply this model to families, to schools, to society at large?

There are institutions—families, academic institutions, and religious institutions—that have lasted for centuries and fundamentally influenced the development of humanity, changed the world, and seem to have implemented at least some of the interventions described earlier.

Consider the Medici family, for example. The Medici family ruled Florence, in Tuscany, between the fourteenth and seventeenth centuries. The Medicis can be considered the founders of modern banking, transforming money lending—which until then was considered usury—into a respectable profession (Ferguson 2008). In 1397, they founded the Medici Bank, which became Europe's largest bank in the fifteenth century, and supported the family's ascent to power in Florence, where they dominated the city's government for many centuries (and for much of this time they officially remained simple citizens).

The family passionately promoted a liberal and open-minded culture in Florence, where art and humanism could flourish. The Medicis were among the most prominent families inspiring and fostering the *Rinascimento,* the opening phase of the Renaissance—the period of great cultural change and achievement in Europe that spanned the period from the end of the thirteenth century to about 1600, and that marked the transition between the Medieval era and modern Europe. The Medicis also produced four popes (Villari 1894).

Another, contemporary example of a family that had a strong influence on society is the Nehru-Gandhi family in India. Committed to public service, and to helping India's society, despite significant dangers, it has been influential in the Indian National Congress for most of India's history since independence. Three members of the family (Pandit Jawaharlal Nehru, his daughter Indira Gandhi, and her son Rajiv Gandhi) have been prime ministers of India, two of whom (Indira and Rajiv Gandhi) were assassinated.

In the United States, the Kennedy family influenced and shaped the nation's political life and society for more than half a century. Their extensive and continuing passion for and commitment to public service, their political involvement with the Democratic Party, and their contributions to Harvard University's John F. Kennedy School of Government have elevated them to legendary status well beyond the United States.

There are academic institutions that have influenced the development of society for nearly a millennium. The University of Bologna is the oldest continuously operating university in the world; its foundation marked the first use of the word *universitas.* The actual year of its founding is uncertain, but is believed to have been 1088. Historically, the university has been notable for its teaching of values and norms, in the form of canon law (the laws and regulations governing Christian churches) and civil law. It has 23 faculties, and eight branches in Italy and abroad.

Over the centuries, the University of Bologna has brought forward an impressive list of leading thinkers, including the astronomer Nicolaus Copernicus, the poet Dante Alighieri, the philosopher Giovanni Pico della Mirandola, and the writer Umberto Eco.

The University of Oxford is also one of the oldest surviving universities, and is regarded as one of the world's leading academic institutions. Although the exact date of its foundation is also unclear, there is evidence of teaching in Oxford as far back as the eleventh century. Most undergraduate teaching at Oxford is organized around tutorials in self-governing cells (colleges and halls), supported by lectures and laboratory classes organized by the university's faculties and departments.

Oxford consistently ranks among the world's top 10 universities. There is a long list of notable alumni (called Oxonians) including 26 British prime ministers (among them Margaret Thatcher, Tony Blair, and David Cameron), one U.S. president (Bill Clinton), two prime ministers of India, and several leading economists and philosophers, including Adam Smith, John Locke, and Thomas Hobbes.

Finally, the Roman Catholic Church is both the largest and the oldest continuously operating institution in the Western world, having existed in its current form since the fourth century. The Church defines its mission as spreading the gospel of Jesus Christ, administering the sacraments, and exercising charity. It operates social programs and institutions throughout the world, including schools, universities, hospitals, missions, shelters, and charities (O'Collins and Farrugia 2003). It is probably the most striking example of a large institution that provides meaning to its members and promotes a strong value system.

The Church's organization, which is very simple and flat, is headed by the Pope. Reporting to the Pope are nearly 3,000 independent performance cells called dioceses, highly autonomous units overseen by a bishop (or in some cases an abbot). Dioceses are divided into individual communities called parishes, each staffed by one or more priests and deacons. All clergy, including deacons, priests, and bishops, may preach, teach, baptize, witness marriages, and conduct funerals.

Despite scandals and setbacks over the many centuries (from the schisms in the Middle Ages to the recent accusations of child abuse by priests in several countries), the Church is a successful and fast-growing organization. In the 1950s the Church had just over 400 million members, in the 1970s it had nearly 700 million members, and today nearly 1.2 billion people are members of the Church (Bazar 2008).

If families, schools, and institutions that shape societies and change the world are a possibility, can we apply our model of the firm that thrives in dynamic markets to create more of them? Can we create more families, schools, and institutions that are driven by a purpose, that lead by learners, that are framed positively, that build on their members' eagerness to perform and learn, that are open to challenge?

Can we teach ourselves, the parents, to be better parents, able to develop our children's capabilities and self-confidence? Can we teach them the values that will enable them to be better people? Can we build the self-confidence our daughters and sons need for tackling the future?

Can we transform our schools from institutions that select the best students by their ability to assimilate scientific information, and academic knowledge, to institutions that, no less than developing academic skills of the pupils, also nurture their curiosity and an eagerness to learn throughout their lives?

Can we build more great institutions in our society?

The answers are obvious.

■ ■ ■

Gwen, Carl, and the kids had a great time in Osaka. The life of an expatriate family is often good for the family's unity. There is a feeling of being in it together, and that was exactly the feeling the Bergers had.

When Carl was appointed to lead AHD, the family moved back to the United States. Unaware of what was awaiting them, they were all happy to be coming back. But the return wasn't as easy as they had imagined it would be.

Dave and Alex were two intelligent young adults who had excelled in the International School in Osaka, but they struggled initially in the United States. It was obviously not a matter of language, since their schooling had always been in English.

It was a matter of self-confidence.

The mind-set of their old school was one of building confidence and character. For example, their teachers would ask the children to give presentations about themselves, and to talk about their hobbies and thoughts in front of the entire class. And they would offer encouraging, positive feedback. At the same time, the school had had a powerful ethos of the importance of education and achievement. Children were expected to perform to a high standard, and congratulated when they did so. Dave and Alex grew up healthy, curious, and full of energy and self-confidence.

The school they now attended was in some ways different. Although it left plenty of space for the development of children's characters, in what it emphasized was a child-centered environment, there was little structure to the curriculum and few expectations as to achievement.

Dave and Alex suffered, and slowly but surely, month after month, their self-confidence declined. They found it difficult to relate to the interests of their new fellow students. They were plagued by doubts. They stopped seeing their friends, often spending time sitting at home playing computer games alone. Their self-confidence vanished; their grades deteriorated.

Family life became very tense. Confronted with Carl's and Gwen's high expectations, the children faltered. It was also a difficult time for Gwen and Carl, who had differing views on how to intervene, if at all.

Carl, who had dropped out of school at the age of 12 and had no high opinion of the school system, felt that the problem was the school. Gwen pinpointed the problem as an issue with individual teachers. Importantly, though, neither of them saw their children as the problem.

But they were perceptive enough to work on giving Dave and Alex more confidence and support, and slowly but surely things started to change. After a year, the children found their feet, their grades got better, they started going out again, they were more cheerful, more positive, more engaged. They had regained their self-confidence.

They blossomed. And the family blossomed.

CHAPTER 13

Legacy through Leadership

O ur reviews of the various academic fields have shown that informed and thoughtful interventions can interrupt or at least slow down the process of aging and decaying of firms.

Organizations that thrive in today's dynamic markets, organizations that are driven by the desire to make a difference, that are led by a team of learners, that are framed positively, that are built on self-managed performance cells that promote their members' drive to perform and grow, that are quick to develop new assets and skills, and that have cultures that foster execution while simultaneously promoting challenge don't happen just by accident. They are acts of human creation.

More precisely, they are acts of leadership. If company leaders do not accept challenge and diverging views, neither will the organization. If company leaders do not show self-confidence, do not have a positive mindset, and do not role-model resilience, the organization will not develop the confidence to adapt to ever-changing and dynamic markets. If company leaders do not change their behavior when confronted with new situations, the company will run on autopilot. If company leaders do not clearly define the structure of the organization and fight organizational complexity, complexity will creep throughout the organization. If company leaders do not thoughtfully review and reward performance, behaviors fostering collaboration and innovation will become rare and—over time—disappear.

Serial innovators, firms that adapt and thrive in dynamic markets, are created by leaders. They are the result of company creations and transformations led by company leaders.

Scott Keller and Colin Price of McKinsey & Company believe that company leaders play a decisive role in such company transformations in four ways.

First, company leaders need to make the transformation journey meaningful to the organization's members. Keller and Price argue that company leaders should develop and tell a personal and engaging change story, a narrative that helps employees believe in the transformation (Keller and Price 2011).

Second, company leaders need to role-model desired mindsets and behaviors. "Everyone in the organization takes their cue from the CEO as to what really matters," say Keller and Price. With their actions, company leaders demonstrate and show what the new types of behavior look like (Keller and Price 2011).

Third, company leaders need to build a strong and committed top team. A company leader can't change an entire organization all by herself. Building a team of trusted, like-minded people is core to any transformation (Keller and Price 2011).

Fourth, company leaders need to relentlessly pursue impact. Keller and Price argue that leaders should focus on what really matters, on where the stake is highest, financially and symbolically. They believe that "there is no substitute for CEOs rolling up their sleeves and getting personally involved," so as to show the entire organization what really matters (Keller and Price 2011).

Creating serial innovators is an ambitious target. But the payout goes beyond creating an organization that can thrive in dynamic markets for long periods of time. Creating serial innovators is also creating a leadership legacy.

The term *leadership legacy* is often referred to in the context of leadership transition, and many academics and scholars have published on the matter, often from different angles. Two recent books focus on the leadership legacy explicitly (Galford and Fazio Maruca 2006; Kouzes and Posner 2006). They define *legacy* as what one wishes to be remembered for after one's departure. A legacy should provide answers to such questions as: How do you wish to be remembered by those inside and outside an organization? For which personal characteristics (values, skills, and behaviors) would you like to be remembered? And they argue that company leaders should write their legacy statements when appointed, and that such legacy statements can be instrumental in helping new leaders focus on what really matters, making them better leaders.

While the question of what you wish to be remembered for may be helpful in some cases, I doubt that it necessarily leads to a legacy that makes a firm stronger. What if the values and behavior of a leader are dysfunctional, and thus place a limitation on the development of the firm? Assume for a moment that a crisis in an organization's industry is an immediate threat. Handling the crisis may require changing to a more hierarchical organization and to a top-down leadership approach. Could a CEO who wants to be remembered for an empowering, bottom-up leadership approach be harmful in such a situation?

Furthermore, legacy statements written as an answer to the question of what people want to be remembered for read like obituaries. That is hardly the type of document that is inspiring to read, let alone to use as a guide for daily decisions.

I would like to offer another concept of leadership legacy, one that has two elements.

First, developing a legacy is building an organization that builds human passion, self-confidence, values, and capabilities.

The organizational model of the serial innovator builds on an image of the human being that has emerged from the various academic reviews that have taken us to behavioral economics, cognitive neuroscience, psychology, network theory, anthropology, organizational science, sociology, and strategy. Reviewing these areas led us to depart from the traditional view of *homo economicus*. The review helped us to paint a new picture (at least for neoclassical economists) of the human being; a human being who is fallible and modestly gifted intellectually; a human being who is naturally insecure and anxious; a human being who can cheat and descend into unsocial and unethical behavior. But it also produced an image of a human being who is deeply inspiring and energizing: a human being who is keen to contribute to something that matters and to make a difference in life; a human being who is motivated by achieving ambitious goals; a human being who is naturally curious, creative, eager to learn and to develop (new synapses); a human being who can be altruistic and social in nature; a human being who can develop the self-confidence and perseverance to achieve greatness in life.

Inspired by the mission statement of the Stanford Graduate School of Business, which aims to ". . . develop innovative, principled, and insightful leaders who change the world," building a leadership legacy is building a firm that develops individuals who are individually and collectively passionate and energized to contribute to something bigger, to something that matters, and to make a difference in life; it develops individuals who are motivated to achieve ambitious goals; individuals who have the self-confidence and perseverance to master difficult challenges; it develops individuals who are open to challenge and eager to learn; individuals who are principled; individuals who can change the world.

Second, developing a legacy is building an organization that has a positive impact on society. It is building an organization that—with its mission, values, and scale—continuously invents new products and services that make life healthier, better, safer; an organization that can change the world.

Take two examples: Ford and Apple. With the introduction of the Model T in 1908, a simple and affordable car, Henry Ford revolutionized transportation and American society in the last century. Driven by a vision of making cars an affordable means of transportation for everyone, he broke new ground in automobile development and manufacturing. He developed a simple, highly standardized car ("Any customer can have a car painted any color that he wants as long as it is black," Ford wrote in his autobiography). And he was intensely committed to continuously lowering costs, which led to many innovations, including the introduction of the moving assembly belt in mass production and of the franchise system that put a car dealership in every city in the United States.

Steve Jobs, the co-founder, chairman, and former chief executive officer of Apple, is one of the world's most admired business leaders. With his vision of bringing high technology to consumers by developing products that are both functional and elegant, Steve Jobs has changed the way we use our personal computers, mobile phones, and portable music devices. His vision of "Think Different," his aspiration and intense commitment to positioning Apple at the forefront of information technology by foreseeing trends (Jobs once said: "There's an old Wayne Gretzky quote that I love. 'I skate to where the puck is going to be, not where it has been.' And we've always tried to do that at Apple.") has led to many breakthrough innovations such as the Macintosh computer, the iMac, the iPod, the iPhone, and the iPad.

Henry Ford co-founded the Ford Motor Company over a century ago, in 1903. Steve Jobs co-founded Apple over 35 years ago, in 1976. As visionaries, as committed and passionate leaders, Henry Ford and Steve Jobs have built organizations that—beyond creating shareholder value—have fundamentally changed their industries, and society. These organizations have changed the world, and created value not only for their shareholders, but also for their customers, and for society.

With the Ford Motor Company and Apple—Henry Ford and Steve Jobs made a difference in life at scale. They have built leadership legacies.

■ ■ ■

At AHD's headquarters on Values Day in 2011, Hubert gave the keynote speech. Of course, he made the point that AHD was a very healthy company. But he then went on to spell out what he meant by "healthy."

"I no longer recognize this company," he said. "We now live our mission, have a winning business model, have a strong team at the top, have a flat organization. And we have a culture that has replaced suspicion with trust, cynicism with commitment, and a focus just on the numbers with a focus above all on our clients.

"I would like to thank Carl, on all our behalf, for all that he has done to transform AHD."

Listening to Hubert's words, Carl realized that, while he had not set out deliberately to transform AHD, that is what had happened. He had set out to understand what mattered to people (including himself) and why they behaved the way they did. Now, it appeared that combining his discoveries with a determination to do what seemed the right thing (plus some luck along the way) had indeed transformed AHD.

When AHD's annual report for 2010 came out, one analyst at a large Wall Street bank noted: "With its diversified product range, its strong pipeline, its position in many of the fast-growing markets in the world, and its cash-generating operating model, AHD is optimally positioned to be the winner in the dynamic medical device industry for the decade to come."

The stock was recommended as a *strong buy*.

Carl took the analysis home to share with Gwen. Talking with her over a glass of wine, he could voice his satisfaction that, with AHD, he had developed a piece of his personal legacy. He explained that now he knew he would eventually hand his successor a firm with all the intrinsic resources it needed to remain a lighthouse firm long into the future.

Also, Carl's health situation improved. His research and energy hadn't been solely focused on building AHD into a vibrant, vital, and growing organization. He also kept up to date on cancer research. And he approached the treatment of his cancer with the same thoughtfulness and scientific attitude as he approached everything else in his life.

On the journey of searching for the right answers, he worked with several oncologists, encouraging diverging opinions and debate. He adopted a learning mind-set and approached every setback—and during treatment, there are many—as a learning experience. Thoughtful choices and luck—the good fortune that novel medicaments kept being discovered and developed—helped.

His oncologists now believe that Carl may live a reasonably long life, and—considering the fast pace of biomedical discovery—maybe even a normally long life.

Gwen and Carl bought a house in Tuscany.

Afterword

Carl was a lucky man. He was lucky as leader. What would have happened if the board had voted differently on the future of the OPEN strategy? What would have happened if he had not met the behavioral psychology professor on the flight to Zurich? What if he had not received the insightful note on AHD's complex organization written by a courageous new employee?

He was lucky as a father and husband. What would have happened if the kids had continued to struggle in school? What if their self-confidence had vanished? What if that had led them into another, maybe less positive direction?

And Carl was lucky as a cancer patient. What if his disease had been discovered much later, with significantly more widespread metastases? What if the novel therapies that helped him had never been discovered? Carl's story as a cancer patient is a story with a happy ending. Unfortunately, not all stories about cancer have such an ending.

Cancer is a terrible disease. Thanks to the enormous progress of pharmaceutical research in the past two decades, some types of cancer have become well treatable, especially if detected early. For some types of cancer, however, the survival rates continue to be low, too low.

One in three individuals is diagnosed with cancer in the course of a lifetime; 15 percent of all deaths are due to cancer. But cancer doesn't affect only the individuals diagnosed with the disease. The enormous psychological weight, the pain of the chemotherapy that often follows the diagnosis, and the fear of death also affect individuals close to the patients: their partner, wife or husband, their children, their relatives, their friends.

I hope that by offering this story of a cancer patient with a happy ending I do not offend or hurt the feelings of anyone affected by cancer, patients, or individuals close to them, who may be less fortunate than Carl.

But, you may ask, what has the story of a cancer patient to do with individual and organizational rigidities? Why, you may wonder, did I choose to tell the story of an ambitious young man, who, when confronted with death, comes to recognize that an element of his legacy is the enduring impact that he has on his organization and on society?

In using the story of a cancer patient I wanted to make one point, a point that I felt strongly and vividly when interviewing people who at some stage in their lives were or still are affected by a potentially terminal disease. The point is to live a life that matters, a life in which we make a difference.

This point came to me when—during the research for this book—I visited Abbot Martin of the Monastery of Einsiedeln. I have known Abbot Martin since 2006, when McKinsey & Company served the monastery on a pro bono project. I am not religious. My parents were atheists, I never went to church, and I do not believe in God. But I believe that if one can help less-privileged people, one should help them. I feel an obligation to help institutions that support less-privileged individuals, or that operate schools and prepare children for their adult life. This monastery does both.

Abbot Martin invited me to stay for lunch with the 50 or so monks of the monastery. I thought that a lunch with the monks might be interesting and fun. Abbot Martin is an interesting and very thoughtful person, so I was expecting a vivid and interesting discussion with the monks, but I was disappointed. Nobody spoke. Not one word.

We ate in a very big room, with a high ceiling full of marvelous paintings. In the room there was a very long, U-shaped table, maybe 40 meters long and 20 meters wide. All the monks sat in complete silence at the exterior side of the table, so that they were not facing anyone closely. The lunch lasted for roughly an hour, and during that hour the only noise in the room came from the table reader and from the cutlery touching the china dishes.

It seemed as if the monks were immersed in their thoughts, as if they were meditating. Then I noticed something weird. Each of them had a little box for his cutlery to the right of his dish. The box was black and was in the shape of a coffin. On each of the coffins there was a cross. It looked macabre.

After the lunch, I shared my observations with Abbot Martin. I told him that I found the coffins to be quite macabre. He smiled at me and said: "Claudio, we Benedictine monks believe that only if one faces death does one understand the importance of living a life that matters. The coffin serves as a daily reminder that one day we all die. It helps us to focus our thoughts and actions on what really matters, on doing good, on helping others grow. For instance, in our school we prepare children for adulthood. We give them self-confidence; we help them discover their passions; we teach them skills; we teach them to help others; we teach values. With that, they can go and change the world."

In building institutions that develop passionate, principled, self-confident, learning individuals, we can do good, too. With our words and our actions, we can have an impact on other people. We can help them discover their true passions; we can help them build their self-confidence; we can help them develop their curiosity and learning capabilities; we can teach values; we can have an impact on society.

Parents have the opportunity to do this every day with their children, teachers with their students, coaches with their sport teams.

Leaders of organizations—teams, departments, divisions, companies, larger institutions—have the opportunity to do so with hundreds, thousands, and sometimes millions, of people. They can "do good at scale." They can have lasting impact. They can change the world.

Analysis of the Top 50 U.S. Firms of 1960

In this appendix, we look at the development of the top 50 U.S. firms of 1960. In particular we are interested to understand which firms have retained their top 50 status in 2010, which existing firms have lost their top 50 status, and which firms no longer exist.

1960 Rank	Company	2010 Top 50 (Rank)	No Longer in Top 50 Rank	Filed Bankruptcy or Has Been Taken Over	Comment
1	General Motors	8			On June 8, 2009, General Motors (GM) filed for reorganization under the provisions of Chapter 11, Title 11, United States Code. On July 10, 2009, with financing partially provided by the U.S. government, GM emerged from reorganization. GM was re-listed on the NYSE on November 18, 2010. The U.S. and Canadian governments acquired a major stake of GM shares.
2	Exxon Mobil[1]	2			
3	Ford Motor	10			
4	General Electric	6			
5	U.S. Steel		X		
6	Mobil			X	On November 30, 1999, Exxon and Mobil joined to form ExxonMobil Corporation.
7	Chrysler			X	Chrysler entered into a partnership dubbed a "merger of equals" with German-based Daimler-Benz AG in 1998 creating the combined entity DaimlerChrysler AG. Daimler subsequently acquired Chrysler.
8	Texaco			X	Merged with Chevron in 2001 to form ChevronTexaco and renamed to Chevron in 2005.

#	Company				Notes
9	Gulf Oil			X	Merged with Chevron in 1984. However, the Gulf brand name and a number of the constituent business divisions of Gulf Oil survived. Gulf, in its present incarnation, is a "New Economy" business. The rights to the brand in the United States are owned by Gulf Oil Limited Partnership (GOLC), which is a wholly owned subsidiary of Cumberland Farms and operates over 2,100 service stations and several petroleum terminals.
10	AT&T Technologies	12			
11	Esmark			X	Acquired by Beatrice Foods in 1984.
12	Bethlehem Steel			X	Filed bankruptcy by 2001 and sold to International Steel Group in 2003.
13	DuPont		X		
14	Amoco			X	Merged with BP in 1998.
15	General Dynamics		X		
16	CBS		X		
17	Shell Oil				Integrated into Royal Dutch Shell.[2]
18	Armour			X	Acquired by Greyhound Corporation in 1970.
19	Navistar International		X		
20	Kraft	49			
21	Chevron	3			
22	Boeing	36			
23	Goodyear		X		
24	Union Carbide			X	Acquired by Dow Chemical in 2001.
25	RCA			X	Acquired by General Electric in 1986.
26	Procter & Gamble	26			

(Continued)

173

1960 Rank	Company	2010 Top 50 (Rank)	No Longer in Top 50 Rank	Filed Bankruptcy or Has Been Taken Over	Comment
27	IBM	18			
28	Lockheed Martin[3]		X		Lockheed Martin Corporation was formed in March 1995 with the merger of Lockheed Corporation and Martin Marietta Corporation.
29	Sinclair Oil		X		
30	Firestone			X	Acquired by Japanese Bridgestone Corporation in 1988.
31	ConocoPhillips[4]	4			ConocoPhillips was created through the merger of Conoco Inc. and the Phillips Petroleum Company in 2002.
32	GTE	16			GTE merged with Bell Atlantic in 2000, and named the new entity Verizon Communications.
33	Douglas Aircraft			X	Merged to McDonnell Douglas with McDonnell Aircraft Corporation in 1967. McDonnell Douglas later merged with Boeing in 1997.
34	Sperry			X	Merged to Unisys with Burroughs in 1986.
35	Continental Group[5]			X	Acquired by Suiza Foods Corporation in 1998.
36	General Foods			X	Acquired by Philip Morris Companies in 1985.
37	American Can			X	American Can Company renamed to Primerica in 1997, after divesting the packaging arm in 1986.
38	American Motors			X	Acquired by Renault in 1993.
39	Republic Steel			X	In 1984, Republic Steel merged into the Jones and Laughlin Steel subsidiary of the LTV Corporation, with the new entity being known as LTV Steel. In December 2001, LTV filed for Chapter 11 bankruptcy.

#	Company			Notes
40	International Paper	X		
41	United Technologies[6]	44		
42	Citgo Petroleum		X	Acquired by PDV America, Inc., an indirect wholly owned subsidiary of Petróleos de Venezuela, S.A.
43	Uniroyal		X	Acquired by Michelin in 1990.
44	Rockwell	X	X	Split into Rockwell Automation and Rockwell Collins—both publicly traded companies—in 2001.
45	Borden Chemical		X	Acquired by Kohlberg Kravis Roberts in 1995.
46	Eastman Kodak	X		
47	ARMCO		X	Merged with AK Steel in 1999.
48	Burlington		X	Acquired by International Textile Group in 2003.
49	Monsanto	X		
50	Alcoa	X		

[1] Refers to Exxon.
[2] Through most of Shell's history, its business in the United States, Shell Oil Company was substantially independent with its stock ("Shell Oil") being traded on the NYSE. In the 1990s Shell bought the shares in Shell Oil that it did not own. CNN Money does not count Shell Oil as a U.S. firm anymore.
[3] Refers to Lockheed.
[4] Refers to Phillips Petroleum.
[5] Refers to Continental Can.
[6] Refers to United Aircraft.
Source: CNN Money, company websites.

APPENDIX B

Corporate Aging and Survival

I n this appendix, we review the relevant literature on corporate aging and survival.

Aging, corporate life cycle, and company survival are themes that have received considerable attention by economists over the past three centuries. The relevant literature on corporate aging goes as far back as to the classical economists Adam Smith and David Ricardo (Loderer, Neusser, and Waelchli 2009).

Many economists have observed that companies do well when they are young (Schumpeter 1976; Foster and Kaplan 2001; Loderer, Neusser, and Waelchli 2009). Created on the back of an idea, or of an innovation, the companies capture wealth creation opportunities that develop in the marketplace. The companies learn how to grow and to extract value. They become more efficient, they find ways to standardize their processes, ways to specialize roles in the organization, ways to better market to different customer groups, ways to expand geographically. They build knowledge, skills, capabilities.

However, as firms age their development slows, they lose their vitality and momentum. They seem to develop structural and process-related rigidities, and their knowledge, their skills, their capabilities become obsolete (Leonard-Barton 1992; Loderer, Neusser, and Waelchli 2009). Margins decline, costs increase, profitability deteriorates. "Investments and learning are apparently unable to overcome the deleterious effects of obsolescence" (Loderer, Neusser, and Waelchli 2009).

In their book *Creative Destruction,* Dick Foster and Sarah Kaplan from McKinsey & Company have demonstrated that young firms have an *attacker advantage* (Foster and Kaplan 2001).

Their sample included data of 1,008 large U.S. firms in 15 industries over a period of a little more than three and a half decades (1962 to 1998). By the end of 1998 these 1,008 firms represented USD 2.1 trillion in sales, and USD 5.2 trillion in market capitalization. Foster and Kaplan measured performance with the total return to shareholders created by companies relative to their own industry average.

They found that young firms—new entrants as they called them—outcompete older firms achieving superior total return to shareholders. Eventually, as firms age, performance deteriorates, and roughly after 15 years of age (years after the companies have been included in the sample), total returns to shareholder of the aging firms starts to lag the industry average.

Foster and Kaplan gave three reasons for this pattern of decreasing returns to shareholders relative to industry peers as firms age. First, competitors and even newer entrants start to copy the business ideas and innovations that the original new entrants brought to the market, leaving to them little margins and profitability. Second, valuations of new entrants begin to approach the cost of equity for the industry, as investors learn how to properly value the innovators. Third, aging firms lose momentum and are unable to deliver innovation and create new opportunities on the scale required to maintain an edge on younger firms (Foster and Kaplan 2001).

The findings of Foster and Kaplan have been validated by the work of three economists of the University of Berne, Claudio Loderer, Klaus Neusser, and Urs Waelchli. Their sample included all firms with data on CRSP, COMPUSTAT, and COMPUSTAT Industry Segment between 1978 and 2004, excluding firms with total sales of less than USD 20 million, and firms with either missing or inconsistent data. All in all, their sample included 10,930 firms. They defined firm age as the number of years since listing and before exit. The three economists chose listing as the start date, arguing that listing is a defining moment in a firm's development: it affects ownership, it provides funding to tap into growth opportunities, it increases exposure to various stakeholders such as media, the public, and to a larger number of shareholders. The defined exit as situations—either bankruptcies or takeovers—in which firms cease to exist as legally independent and listed companies. They measured actual financial performance with return on assets (ROA) and market's expectations about future performance with Tobin's Q (market value of the firm's assets divided by their book value) (Loderer, Neusser, and Waelchli 2009).

Figures B.1 and B.2 summarize their findings on the relation between age and corporate performance. They confirm that performance decreases as companies become older.

Figure B.1 depicts company financial performance measured by ROA in relation to company age. Performance of a young firm is above average, and

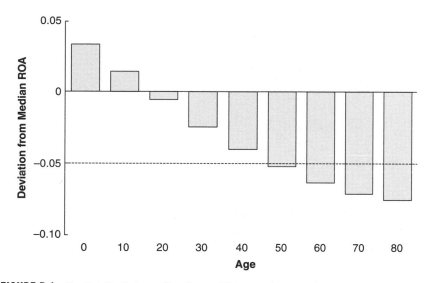

FIGURE B.1 The Relation between Firm Age and Return on Assets

Data source: Loderer, C., K. Neusser, and U. Waelchli 2009. *Corporate Geriatrics: Aging, Survival, and Performance.* Berne, Switzerland: University of Berne, research paper.

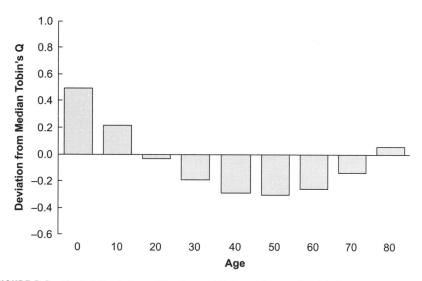

FIGURE B.2 The Relation between Firm Age and Expected Returns (Tobin's Q)

Data source: Loderer, C., K. Neusser, and U. Waelchli 2009. *Corporate Geriatrics: Aging, Survival, and Performance.* Berne, Switzerland: University of Berne, research paper.

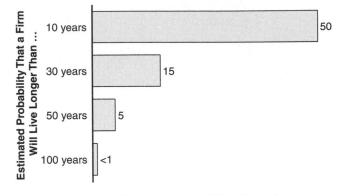

FIGURE B.3   The Relation between Firm Age and Probability of Survival

Data source: Loderer, C., K. Neusser, and U. Waelchli 2009. *Corporate Geriatrics: Aging, Survival, and Performance.* Berne, Switzerland: University of Berne, research paper.

stays so for nearly 15 years. This is consistent with Foster and Kaplan: Firms perform well when they are young. However, after the 15-year mark companies start to underperform and their performance continues to deteriorate further as they grow older.

Figure B.2 depicts expected company performance measured by Tobin's Q in relation to company age. Again, young firms do well. However, it appears that performance rises again at old age. It starts to improve 47 years after the listing.

However, very few firms experience that. Figure B.3 shows the probability of survival in relation to age. Only 5 percent of firms are expected to survive past year 50.

Key Questions for Transforming Your Firm

In this appendix, we summarize the key questions a leader should ask when embarking on a journey to transform a firm into a serial innovator. The questions are discussed under nine themes:

1. Understanding of context

2. Company purpose

3. Top team composition

4. Positive frame

5. Organization

6. Performance management systems

7. Leadership development

8. Capability building

9. Corporate culture

Understanding of Context

Different firms may need different interventions, as context can vary widely from firm to firm. The transformation journey for a 100-year-old insurance company will differ from that of a Silicon Valley software firm. The journey for a firm in a crisis and facing bankruptcy will be different from one for a firm that is operating successfully.

Firms may be exposed to different *market and company dynamics,* they may face different *expectations,* they may have different heritages or *endowments,* and *leaders' beliefs and style* may differ. Key questions may include:

Market and Company Dynamics
- What is the industry context?
- What challenges is the company facing?
- What are the opportunities and the risks?
- What is the track record financial momentum of the company?

Stakeholder Expectations
- What are the expectations of customers or customer groups?
- What are the expectations of shareholders? What do key investors expect? What are the concerns of buy-side and sell-side analysts?
- What are the expectations of the board of directors and those of individual members?
- What are the expectations of employees and top management? Others?
- What are the expectations of regulators and other authorities?

Endowments
- What is the history of the corporation? What were phases of development of the organization? Who were the key leaders, and how did they influence these phases?
- What is the starting position in regard to the firm's capabilities? What is the company good at? What are key deficiencies?
- Who are the key people in the organization? In the management? In other key areas?
- What is the culture of the organization? What are the values in terms of execution and renewal?

Beliefs and Values of the Leaders
- What do I believe is the right strategy forward? Why do I believe it? On what assumptions am I basing my thinking? Are these assumptions correct? What would happen if they were wrong?
- What do I value? Why? Which of my values are helpful, given the journey I want to embark upon? Which ones aren't?

Company Purpose

Many organizations have a sound mission statement, and often a new leader may just need to reaffirm it, and to bring it to life with her own *inspiring stories and metaphors, and by using emotions.* Company leaders may need to reaffirm the company's mission by *visibly committing* to it beyond words. This means visibly investing leadership time, incurring costs, or forgoing gains in adhering to the firm's mission. Key questions may include:

- What is the purpose of the organization?
- Is it altruistic?
- Are the organization's members aligned on the purpose? Are they engaged?
- How is the purpose conveyed to the members of the organization? What stories and metaphors do we use?
- What are examples of actions that make our purpose credible?
- How do we engage the organization's members in debating the purpose of the organization?

Top Team Composition

We have seen that it is essential to have people with diverse mental models, people with a strong belief in their own self-efficacy, and people whose purpose is aligned with that of the firm, staffed in positions that are important for the company in adapting to changes in its environment. Getting the composition and the dynamics of the top team right is likely to be a central part of the transformation journey. Key questions may include:

- Do the members of the top team have a strong individual and collective sense of self-efficacy?
- Do members of the top team have a positive attitude toward learning?
- Do members of the top team have diverse mental models, diverse experiences?
- Can the individual team members work in teams?
- What are missing characteristics in the top team?
- Who are people that may not fit the future top team, and how would the organization compensate capabilities that would be lost should they be removed?

Positive Context

Developing an engaging and convincing strategy, a plan for the years to come, serves two purposes. First, and vitally, the firm has to be successful. A firm that doesn't capture value creation opportunities, in the short and in the long run, is a weak firm that will not last for very long. The second essential purpose is to provide direction to the members of an organization. As we have seen earlier, the members of an organization are more likely to engage in problem-solving and behavioral change that happens in a positively loaded emotional context. Questions may include:

- What is the strategy of the organization?
- Is the strategy coherent and convincing? Why or why not?
- What is the understanding of the strategy in the organization?
- Do organizational members feel energized by the strategy? Are they engaged? Why or why not?

Organization

Organizational design is important, and can be used to improve effectiveness and adaptability of an organization significantly. Key questions may include:

- Is the organization today perceived as effective? Is the organization quick to adapt to new challenges? Is the organization innovative? Is the organization perceived to be slow and bureaucratic? If so, where exactly?
- Are we thoughtful about the organization's objectives? What are the primary objectives, and what should therefore be the dominant axes of management—functional, product, customer, or geography? What should be secondary objectives?
- Can we simplify the organization by breaking it up into self-managed performance cells?
- Can we use knowledge networks to support the organization in achieving secondary objectives?
- Are roles and processes standardized?

Performance Management Systems

Performance management processes play a key role in company adaptation by setting ambitious but achievable goals, using individualized performance feedback, and using both monetary and nonmonetary incentives to reward its members. Questions may include:

- Is the performance and reward system regarded as being effective today?
- How are targets in the corporation set? Are they considered generally ambitious but achievable?
- How is the performance review process structured? Are people compared to others, or are they measured against their own objectives?
- How does the organization use monetary rewards?
- Where and how does it complement them with nonmonetary ones?

Leadership Development

Setting ambitious but achievable goals, providing individualized feedback, managing nonmonetary rewards, but also leading autonomous performance cells requires experience and leadership capabilities. Key questions may include:

- Is the leadership bench of the organization generally considered strong? Based on what benchmarks?
- What is the approach used for development of leadership capabilities?
  - Selection?
  - On-the-job training?
  - Formal training?
  - Assignment planning and rotation?
  - Others?
- Are succession plans in place? To what level in the organization?

Capability Building

A firm is restricted in the wealth-creation opportunities it can capture. At any one time, its existing assets and skills, and the velocity with which it develops new ones, determine its opportunities. Questions may include:

- What approaches exist in the organization to quickly scale up new capabilities?
- What alliances, partnerships, or licensing agreements could be done?

- How could we close gaps by hiring new people, procuring additional technologies, or acquiring entire companies?
- How can the organization experiment by making, for example, venture investments, or by pursuing several smaller strategic moves in areas of potential interest?

Corporate Culture

A corporate culture is likely more effective when it makes use of values and cultural norms that foster both execution and innovation, or execution and renewal. Key questions may include:

- What are the desired execution and renewal values and norms that we wish to install in the organization?
- How would we instill new values and norms using . . .
    - Communication?
    - Formal mechanism (for example, formal processes, incentives, and so on)?
    - Training?
    - Role modeling?

References

Ashkenas, R. 2007. "Simplicity-Minded Management." *Harvard Business Review* 85 (12): 101–109.

Baghai, M., S. Coley, and D. White. 1999. *The Alchemy of Growth: Kickstarting and Sustaining Growth in Your Company*. London: Orion Business Books.

Bandura, A. 1977. *Social Learning Theory*. Englewood Cliffs, NJ: Prentice-Hall.

———. 1982. "Self-Efficacy Mechanism in Human Agency." *American Psychologist* 37:122–147.

———. 1997. *Self-Efficacy: The Exercise of Control*. New York: W. H. Freeman.

Bazar, E. 2008. " Immigrants Make Pilgrimage to Pope." *USA Today*, April 16.

Beinhocker, E. D. 2006. *The Origin of Wealth: Evolution, Complexity, and the Radical Remaking of Economics*. Boston: Harvard Business School Press.

Bolte Taylor, J. 2008. *My Stroke of Insight*. London: Hodder & Stoughton.

Bryan, L. L., and C. I. Joyce. 2005. "The 21st-Century Organization." *The McKinsey Quarterly*, 3.

———. 2007. *Mobilizing Minds: Creating Wealth from Talent in the 21st-Century Organization*. New York: McGraw-Hill.

Coase, R. H. 1937. "The Nature of the Firm." *Economica* 4 (16): 386–405.

Collins, J. C. *How the Mighty Fall*. New York: Random House Business Books, 2009.

Collins, J. C., and J. I. Porras. 1994. *Built to Last: Successful Habits of Visionary Companies*. New York: HarperBusiness.

———. 1996. "Building Your Company's Vision." *Harvard Business Review* 74 (5): 65–78.

Daft, R. L. 2007. *Organization Theory and Design*, 9th ed. Mason, OH: South-Western Cengage Learning.

Denison, D. R. 1990. *Corporate Culture and Organizational Effectiveness.* New York: John Wiley & Sons.

Deutschman, A. 2005. "Change or Die." *Fast Company,* May 1.

Dineen, B. R., R. J. Lewicki, and E. C. Tomlinson. "Supervisory Guidance and Behavioral Integrity: Relationships with Employee Citizenship and Deviant Behavior." *Journal of Applied Psychology* 91 (3) (2006): 622–635.

Dobbs, R., and T. Koller. 2005. "Measuring Long-Term Performance." *McKinsey on Finance* 16.

Fehr, E., and A. Falk. 2002. "Psychological Foundations of Incentives." *European Economic Review* 46:687–724.

Fehr, E., and S. Gächter. 2000. "Cooperation and Punishment in Public Good Experiments." *American Economic Review* 90 (4): 980–994.

Ferguson, N. 2009. *The Ascent of Money: A Financial History of the World.* New York: Penguin Books.

Fogel, R. W. 2000. *The Fourth Great Awakening and the Future of Egalitarianism.* Chicago: University of Chicago Press.

Foster, R., and S. Kaplan. 2001. *Creative Destruction.* New York: Doubleday.

Frankl, V. 1984. *Man's Search for Meaning.* New York: Washington Square Books.

Frisch, B. 2008. "When Teams Can't Decide." *Harvard Business Review* 86 (11): 121–126.

Galford, R. M., and R. Fazio Maruca. 2006. *Your Leadership Legacy: Why Looking towards the Future Will Make You a Better Leader Today.* Boston: Harvard Business School Press.

Gazzaniga, M. S. 1998. *The Mind's Past.* Berkeley: University of California Press.

Gist, M. E. 1987. "Self-Efficacy: Implications for Organizational Behavior and Human Resource Management." *The Academy of Management Review* 12 (3): 472–485.

Gneezy, U., and A. Rustichini. 2000. "Pay Enough or Don't Pay at All." *Quarterly Journal of Economics* 115 (2): 791–810.

Haggbloom, S. J. 2002. "The 100 Most Eminent Psychologists of the 20th Century." *Review of General Psychology* 6 (2): 139–152.

Hannan, M. T., and J. Freeman. 1977. "The Population Ecology of Organizations." *American Journal of Sociology* 82 (5): 929–964.

———. 1989. *Organizational Ecology.* Cambridge, MA: Harvard University Press.

Harder, J. 1999. *Primer on Organizational Culture.* Charlottesville, VA: Darden Business Publishing.

Heifetz, R., A. Grashow, and M. Linsky. 2009. *The Practice of Adaptive Leadership: Tools and Tactics for Changing Your Organization and the World*. Boston: Harvard Business School Press.

Herb, E., K. Leslie, and C. Price. 2001. "Teamwork at the Top." *The McKinsey Quarterly* 2.

Heywood, S., J. Spungin, and D. Turnbull. 2007. "Cracking the Complexity Code." *The McKinsey Quarterly* 2.

Hughes, D. 2004. "NAB Chief Urges Staff to Share the Vision." *The Sydney Morning Herald*, May 22.

Kahneman, D. 2002. " Maps of Bounded Rationality: A Perspective on Intuitive Judgment and Choice." Nobel Prize Lecture, Stockholm, Sweden, December 8.

Kaplan, R. S., and D. P. Norton. 1992. "The Balanced Scorecard—Measures That Drive Performance." *Harvard Business Review*. January–February: 71–79.

Keller, S., M. Kruyt, and J. Malan. 2010. *How Do I Develop an Effective Top Team?* New York: McKinsey & Company.

Keller, S., and C. Price. 2011. *Beyond Performance: How Great Organizations Build Ultimate Competitive Advantage*. Hoboken, NJ: John Wiley & Sons.

Klein, A. 2008. "Organizational Culture as a Source of Competitive Advantage." *E-Leader Bangkok*: 1–10.

Kouzes, J., and B. Posner. 2006. *A Leader's Legacy*. Hoboken, NJ: John Wiley & Sons.

Lawson, E., and C. Price. 2003. "The Psychology of Change Management." *The McKinsey Quarterly* 2: 30–41.

Leonard-Barton, D. 1992. "Core Capabilities and Core Rigidities: A Paradox in Managing New Product Development." *Strategic Management Journal* 13: 111–125.

Levitt, S. D., and S. J. Dubner. 2005. *Freakonomics: A Rogue Economist Explores the Hidden Side of Everything*. New York: William Morrow.

Linden, D. J. 2010. *The Accidental Mind: How Brain Evolution Has Given Us Love, Memory, Dreams, and God*. Berlin, Germany: Rowohlt Verlag.

Loderer, C., K. Neusser, and U. Waelchli. 2009. *Corporate Geriatrics: Aging, Survival, and Performance*. Berne, Switzerland: University of Berne, research paper.

Loderer, C., and U. Waelchli. 2009. *Firm Age and Performance*. Berne, Switzerland: University of Berne, research paper.

Lovallo, D. P., and D. Kahneman. 2003. "Delusions of Success: How Optimism Undermines Executives' Decisions." *Harvard Business Review* 81 (7): 56–63.

Lovallo, D. P., and O. Sibony. 2006. "Distortions and Deceptions in Strategic Decisions." *The McKinsey Quarterly* 1.

Maeda, J. 2006. *The Laws of Simplicity*. Cambridge, MA: MIT Press.

Mallak, L. 2001. "Understanding and Changing Your Organization's Culture." *Industrial Management* 43 (2): 18–24.

Marx, K. 1976. " Introduction to a Contribution to the Critique of Hegel's Philosophy of Right." In Marx and Engels, *Collected Works, 3*. New York: International Publishers.

Mgbere, O. 2009. "Exploring the Relationship between Organizational Culture, Leadership Styles and Corporate Performance: An Overview." *Journal of Strategic Management Education* 5 (3&4): 187–202.

Miller, G. A. 1956. "The Magical Number Seven, Plus or Minus Two: Some Limits on Our Capacity for Processing Information." *Psychological Review* 63 (2): 81–97.

Mitroff, I., and E. Denton. 1999. *A Spiritual Audit of Corporate America*. Hoboken, NJ: Jossey-Bass.

Newberg, A., E. G. D'Aquili, and V. Rause. 2001. *Why God Won't Go Away: Brain Science and the Biology of Belief*. New York: Ballantine Books.

O'Collins, G., and M. Farrugia. 2003. *Catholicism*. New York: Oxford University Press.

Ouchi, W. G. 1981. *Theory Z: How American Business Can Meet the Japanese Challenge*. Reading, MA: Addison-Wesley.

Page, S. E. 1996. "Two Measures of Difficulty." *Economic Theory* 8: 321–346.

Penrose, E. E. T. 1959. *The Theory of the Growth of the Firm*. New York: John Wiley & Sons.

Peters, T. J., and R. H. Waterman Jr. 1982. *In Search of Excellence: Lessons from America's Best-Run Companies*. New York: Warner Books.

Peterson, S. J., and F. Luthans. 2006. "The Impact of Financial and Nonfinancial Incentives on Business-Unit Outcomes over Time." *Journal of Applied Psychology* 91 (1): 156–165.

Pink, D. H. 2006. *A Whole Mind*. New York: Riverhead Books.

Porras, J. I., and B. Anderson. 1981. "Improving Managerial Effectiveness through Modeling-Based Training." *Organizational Dynamics* 9: 60–77.

Porras, J. I., S. Emery, and M. Thompson. 2007. *Success Built to Last*. Philadelphia: Wharton School Publishing.

Porras, J. I., K. Hargis, K. J. Patterson, D. Maxfield, N. Roberts, and R. J. Bies. 1982. "Modeling-Based Organizational Development: A Longitudinal Assessment." *Journal of Applied Behavioral Science* 18: 433–446.

Precht, R. D. 2007. *Who Am I: And If So, How Many? A Philosophical Journey.* Wilhelm Goldmann, trans. Munich, Germany: Verlagsgruppe Random House.

Recardo, R., K. Molloy, and J. Pellegrino. 1995. "How the Learning Organization Manages Change." *National Productivity Review* 15 (1): 7–13.

Reinhart, C. M., and K. S. Rogoff. 2009. *This Time Is Different: Eight Centuries of Financial Folly.* Princeton University Press.

Rock, D., and J. Schwartz. 2006. "The Neuroscience of Leadership." *Strategy+Business* 43 (Summer).

Rosen, R. M., and F. Adair. 2007. "CEOs Misperceive Top Teams' Performance." *Harvard Business Review,* September 1.

Sadri, G., and I. T. Robertson. 1993. "Self-Efficacy and Work-Related Behaviour: A Review and Meta-Analysis." *Applied Psychology: An International Review* 42 (2): 139–152.

Schein, E. H. 1985. *Organizational Culture and Leadership.* Hoboken, NJ: Jossey-Bass.

Schlesinger, A. M. 1965. *A Thousand Days: John F. Kennedy in the White House.* Boston: Houghton Mifflin.

Schumpeter, J. A. 1976. *Capitalism, Socialism and Democracy,* 5th ed. London: George Allen and Unwin.

Schwarzenegger, A. 2004. *Governor Schwarzenegger's State of the State Address.* Sacramento, CA: Office of the Governor of the State of California.

Simon, H. A. 1978. *Rational Decision Making in Business Organizations.* Nobel Memorial Lecture, Stockholm, Sweden, December 8.

Somm, M. 2010. "Gott is ein Hormon." *Die Weltwoche,* Nr. 22.10

Stajkovic, A. D., D. Lee, and A. J. Nyberg. 2009. "Collective Efficacy, Group Potency, and Group Performance: Meta-Analyses of Their Relationships, and Test of a Mediation Model." *Journal of Applied Psychology* 94 (3): 814–828.

Stajkovic, A. D., and F. Luthans. 1997. "A Meta-Analysis of the Effects of Organizational Behavior Modification on Task Performance, 1975–1995." *Academy of Management Journal* 40 (5): 1122–1149.

———. 1998. "Self-Efficacy and Work-Related Performance: A Meta-Analysis." *Psychological Bulletin* 124 (2): 240–261.

Stanford, N. 2007. *Guide to Organizational Design.* London, UK: Profile Books.

Thaler, R. H., and C. R. Sunstein. 2008. *Nudge: Improving Decisions about Health, Wealth, and Happiness.* New Haven, CT: Yale University Press.

Tiger, L., and M. McGuire. 2010. *God's Brain.* Amherst, NY: Prometheus Books.

Turner, M. 1996. *The Literary Mind: The Origins of Thought and Language.* New York: Oxford University Press.

Tversky, A., and D. Kahneman. 1974. "Judgment under Uncertainty: Heuristics and Biases." *Science* 185: 1124–1131.

Villari, P. 1894. " Medici Family." In *Encyclopædia Britannica* 9th ed., vol. 15, 794–804. Philadelphia: Encyclopædia Britannica.

Wiggins, R. R., and T. W. Ruefli. 2005. "Schumpeter's Ghost: Is Hypercompetition Making the Best of Times Shorter?" *Strategic Management Journal* 26: 887–911.

Wood, R. E., and A. Bandura. 1989. "Social Cognitive Theory of Organizational Management." *Academy of Management Review* 14: 361–384.

Acknowledgments

As Colin Price writes in the Prologue of this book, many important innovations and achievements would not have been possible without groups of individuals collaborating effectively and contributing to a common cause. It is certainly true that I could not have written this book alone. I am greatly indebted to the many people who have contributed in many different ways to this book. All mistakes in the book are no doubt mine.

I would like to thank those who have reviewed the manuscript or parts of it and contributed with their ideas, observations, and suggestions (in alphabetical order): Eric Bernheim, Christian Casal, David Court, Kai Eberhardt, Bill Falloon, Ernst Fehr, Marc Feigen, Martin Dewhurst, Rolf Dobelli, Mario Greco, Thomas Gutzwiller, Peter Hahn, Michael Halbye, Doug Haynes, Bill Huyett, Larry Kanarek, Eric Labaye, Shawn Langer, Kevin Lane, Michael Luhnen, Dennis Martinis, Robin Matthias, Paolo Moretti, Tore Myrholt, Michael Ollmann, Colin Price, Sirus Ramezani, Jorge Santos da Silva, Mari Scheiffele, Sven Smit, David Speiser, and Felix Wenger.

For their help on the research for the book, I would like to thank Michael Egli and Florian Graf.

I am greatly indebted to Erika Rauzin and Charles Whitehouse for editing the manuscript and for providing numerous ideas and suggestions on Carl as a character.

I would also like to thank Connie Jordan, Rik Kirkland, and Michael Stewart from McKinsey & Company for their help with internal and external communications and publishing teams.

I am also deeply indebted to the team at John Wiley & Sons that supported me in the past year: Bill Falloon, Meg Freeborn, Mary Daniello, Sharon Polese, Stacy Smith, and Tiffany Charbonier. With their continuous challenge, dedication, relentless support, and hard work, they transformed the manuscript into the book it now is.

Finally, my greatest gratitude is to my family: to my wife Evelyne and to our sons Dario and Alessio, not least for indulging me while I was working on this book during so many evenings and weekends in the past 12 months.

CLAUDIO FESER

About the Author

C laudio Feser is a senior partner of McKinsey & Company, Inc., where he leads the McKinsey CEO Network, a practice that focuses on CEO training and coaching. Before that, from 1999 to 2004, Mr. Feser led the Greek office, and from 2005 to 2010, the Swiss office of McKinsey & Company.

He has counseled the CEOs of some of the world's largest and most renowned companies during his career.

Claudio Feser holds an MS in Business Administration and Economics from the University of Berne, Switzerland, and an MBA from INSEAD, France.

Claudio Feser is married and the father of two sons.

Index